Thomas George Spyers

The Labour Question

An Epitome of the Evidence and the Report of the Royal Commission on Labour

Thomas George Spyers

The Labour Question
An Epitome of the Evidence and the Report of the Royal Commission on Labour

ISBN/EAN: 9783337073817

Printed in Europe, USA, Canada, Australia, Japan

Cover: Foto ©Suzi / pixelio.de

More available books at **www.hansebooks.com**

THE LABOUR QUESTION

AN EPITOME OF THE EVIDENCE AND

THE REPORT OF THE

ROYAL COMMISSION ON LABOUR

BY

T. G. SPYERS, B.A.

(Précis Writer to the Commission)

LONDON

SWAN SONNENSCHEIN & CO.

NEW YORK: CHARLES SCRIBNER'S SONS

1894

PREFACE.

THIS work is an epitome of the evidence collected and the recommendations made by the Royal Commission on Labour. Only part of the evidence was derived from the direct examination of witnesses— 40 of the 65 Blue Books being devoted to other matter. But it is with that part that this volume is chiefly concerned, and to which most of the footnote references are made.

Those references are made in the following manner. The symbol " A " denotes the group of publications connected with the proceedings of Committee A, which dealt with the mining, iron, engineering, hardware, shipbuilding, and cognate trades. The symbol " B " denotes the group of publications connected with the proceedings of Committee B, which dealt with the transport trades. The symbol " C " denotes the group of publications connected with the proceedings of Committee C, which dealt with the textile, clothing, chemical, building, and miscellaneous trades. And the symbol " W " denotes the group of publications connected with the proceedings of the Commission sitting as a whole to examine the representatives of various movements, organisations, and institutions,

Each of these groups of publications comprises one or more volumes of the minutes, which give a full verbatim report of the oral evidence, of appendices, which contain a reprint of the documentary evidence, and of digests, which present the statements made by the witnesses in a continuous narrative form and as modified by the results of cross-examination. The symbols I., II., and III. denote the first, second, and third volumes of minutes, appendices, or digests.

A full list of the publications of the Commission is given in an appendix to the present volume.

CONTENTS.

PART II.

CONDITIONS OF LABOUR.

CHAPTER I.

INDUSTRIAL REMUNERATION.

CHAPTER II.

HOURS OF LABOUR.

CHAPTER III.

EMPLOYERS' LIABILITY.

CHAPTER II.

TRANSPORT TRADES.

CHAPTER III.

AGRICULTURE.

CHAPTER IV.

LABOUR DEPARTMENTS AND LABOUR COUNCILS.

CHAPTER V.

RECOMMENDATIONS OF THE COMMISSION.

THE LABOUR COMMISSION.

PART I.

INDUSTRIAL POLITICS.

CHAPTER I.

THE LABOUR MOVEMENT.

Trade Unionism—Socialism—Co-operation—Relations between
them—The Unity of the Labour Movement.

FIRST among the problems confronting a Commission
appointed to inquire into the "questions raised during
recent trade disputes" was to analyse the force that
had raised them. The evidence, however, scarcely
throws sufficient light on what may be called the
anatomy of the Labour Movement to prove the
following points which it suggests.

✝ The backbone of the movement is obviously Trade
Unionism, or the association of workmen by trades
and districts to improve the conditions under which
they work; but a moment's reflection will show that

A

it is not in Trade Unionism that a proof or an explanation of the solidarity of the movement is to be found. For what is the essence of Trade Unionism? In one word—protection. Every Union exists primarily for the protection of its own members, not only against employers and non-unionist workers, but also against members of other organisations like itself. The evidence from the shipbuilding industry was mainly concerned with the quarrels among the various groups of workmen as to the demarcation of work. Joiners and shipwrights, dockyard labourers and shipbuilders, plumbers and engineers, were said to be constantly at daggers drawn, and their respective Unions to be mainly occupied in conducting and settling their mutual warfare. So, too, in the mining industry; a long feud was said to have subsisted between the local Unions of South Wales miners and the Mining Federation of Great Britain, in consequence of which the members of the rival bodies refused to work in the same pits. Considerable jealousy was also shown to have existed between the North of England and the National Amalgamated Sailors' and Firemen's Unions until 1890, when a *modus vivendi* was fortunately established. All through the evidence, moreover, the policy of the Trade Unions was shown to be entirely self-regarding. Thus, when the representatives of the Amalgamated Society of Engineers spoke of the necessity of absorbing the unemployed, they announced their intention of putting further restrictions on the admission of apprentices to their trade, as a means towards that end. In other words, they contemplated not the employment of the unemployed, but their ex-

clusion from the organisation and industry of the
Amalgamated Society of Engineers. Clearly, therefore, it is not in Trade Unionism alone that the unity
of the Labour Movement is to be found, and it is,
accordingly, desirable to examine the evidence with a
view to discovering what other forces are at work, and
how they are inter-related.

Of these forces, Socialism is perhaps the most important. It may be defined as belief in the blending of
political and industrial functions. It contemplates the
State becoming the sole landlord, the sole capitalist, and
the sole employer of labour. It derives its strength from
the political enfranchisement of the industrial class,
which, as Mr. Sidney Webb pointed out in the course of
his evidence, has naturally had the effect of directing
the action of the State to the solution of industrial
problems.[1]

Another force of a very different nature is Co-
operation, or the association of workmen to become
their own purveyors, or their own employers. Its
success may be said to have originated with the
establishment of the Rochdale Pioneer Society in 1844.
It now embraces no fewer than 1624 societies, which
have an aggregate membership of 1,191,369, control a
capital of over 16 million sterling, and do a trade of
about £50,000,000 a year, at a net profit of nearly
£5,000,000.

Other forces, as exemplified in the Friendly Societies, etc., are at work; but the correlation of these
three—Trade Unionism, Socialism and Co-operation
—is all that the evidence assists us to explain.

[1] W. Dig. p. 19.

First, then, as to the relations between Trade Unionism and Socialism. In many respects, they would
appear to be naturally competing and hostile. The
former represents the interests of each individual
trade or district against those of all the rest, while the
latter represents the interests of all against the interests of each. The fetish of the former is " the trade,"
while the fetish of the latter is "the State." They
approach the problem of industrial politics, the one
from the industrial, the other from the political side.

This inherent antagonism is recognised by many of
the Trade Unions, and often leads them to entertain
the greatest possible mistrust of the interference of
the State in industrial matters. Thus, most of them
have the strongest objection to State regulation of
wages, and many to State Arbitration in trade disputes, while seventeen branches of the Steam Engineers' Society were said to have refused even to discuss the question of a legal eight hours' day on the
ground that it was a political question, and, therefore,
out of order.[1]   Indeed, the Unions that are in favour
of State regulation of certain industrial matters, seem
to desire it only because the workmen disobey or refuse to join them. The typical Trade Unionist spirit
was that which led Mr. Toyn of the Cleveland Miners'
Association to say:—" If an eight hours' day were
given by law, instead of by organised effort, the.wor-
kers would not be persuaded to organise at all."[2]

On the other hand, the Socialists are equally mis-
trustful of the exclusive spirit of the Trade Unions.

[1] A. III. Dig. 39.   Min. 23678-80.
[2] A. I. Min. 1171.

Their opinion on this point was thus summed up by a writer in the *Contemporary Review:*—"No Trade Union is in a position at once to assume irresponsible control of its own industry. Nor would it be tolerable that it should do so. The great engines of our national subsistence are not to be run as the property and for the profit of the engineers any more than for that of private capitalist owners."[1] Mr. Sidney Webb, moreover, in the course of his evidence on the eight hours' day, said :—" If the matter be left to the Trade Unions, an important third party, *viz.*, the public, is deprived of a voice in the transaction. It is quite possible for the Trade Unions and the employers to mutually agree upon a shortening of hours for the express purpose of taxing the public, and an Act of Parliament is the only medium by which the public consent to be so taxed can be expressed."[2]

Yet, with all this antagonism of principle, it is an undeniable fact that many Trades Unions, especially those of recent institution, show a marked preference for using the State machinery instead of their own, and a resolution to the effect that " candidates (for election to the Parliamentary Committee) receiving financial assistance must pledge themselves to support the principles of collective ownership and control of all the means of production and distribution," was carried at the last Trade Union Congress by 137 votes against 97.

Turning to the relations between Trade Unionism and Co-operation, the same antagonism of principle combined with harmony of practice is discernible.

[1] *Contemporary Review*, No. 335, p. 761.
[2] W. Min. 4346-77.

The former is essentially the movement of wages, whereas the latter is essentially the movement of profits. The former tries to increase the wage fund at the expense of the profit fund which the latter gives the workmen an interest in preserving intact. The former opposes the payment by results which forms the basis of the system of the latter. But in spite of this antagonism, both movements are tending to unite their forces. They send delegates to one anothers congresses, instruct their Parliamentary Committees to promote one anothers Bills, and, through the mouth of their representatives, combined to ask the Commission to recommend an alteration in the law with a view to facilitating the investment of Trade Union funds in co-operative enterprises.

An examination of the relations between Socialism and Co-operation will show a similar result. Messrs. Tom Mann,[1] and H. M. Hyndman,[2] whose evidence was mainly devoted to explaining and defending the Socialist idea, agreed in urging the Government to support the co-operative societies, which the complete application of their own principles would destroy, and the representatives of the co-operative societies—not, it is true, without some misgiving—welcomed the proposed alliance.[3]

In fact, these three movements, founded on different principles, with different ideals and different aims, are, nevertheless, all tending to unite.

The force that is welding them together is un-

[1] W. Min. 2375.
[2] W. Min. 8437.
[3] W. Min. 356-405, 654-62, 933-8.

doubtedly the will of the workman, whose patronage they all solicit. Trade Unionism stands highest in his favour, but even Trade Unionism is conscious that she cannot do all the good expected of her unaided. In order to protect her loyal adherents against the disloyalty of the disloyal, she feels bound to join with Socialism in invoking the assistance of the State. She also recognises the impression which the success of Co-operation has made upon her clients, and is not wholly and irreconcilably protectionist. As Sir Thomas Farrer pointed out, she is learning to recognise that the British workman is not merely a producer but a consumer as well.[1] Socialism, moreover, being really a literary movement, frankly recognises the impossibility of reaching the workman except through the Trade Unions. Socialist organisation on non-industrial lines has, indeed, been attempted, but it has never made any great headway among the industrial classes. The Socialist witnesses examined before the Commission accordingly drew a clear distinction between their creed and their programme, and insisted that they did not advocate the complete application of their principles to British industry at the present time. "It must be remembered," said Mr. Mann, "that a limit is placed upon the expediency of extending the functions of any public (*i.e.*, political) authority by the mental and moral make-up of its constituents. The only kind of public authority that can be trusted to realise the collectivist ideal in its completeness is one that is properly representative of a perfectly educated and enlightened community.[2]

[1] W. Min. 7912-27.
[2] W. Dig. p. 17.   Min. 2087-111, 2285.

Socialism needs the support of the co-operative movement also, because it embraces the large number of
industrial establishments that are already in the
hands of the working classes, and is already organised
on a quasi-political plan. " Co-operation," said Mr.
Tom Mann, " is a means of transition towards State
and municipal employment."[1]

The co-operative societies, perhaps, have less to gain
by a policy of alliance ; but they certainly have more
to lose by a policy of isolation. They are themselves
large employers of labour ; but, sometimes from choice,
sometimes from necessity, are excluded from the employers' associations. It is, therefore, a matter of
supreme importance for them to cultivate the security
against strikes which the Trade Unions are offering
them on exceptionally favourable terms. And if the
Trade Unions are Socialist, the co-operative societies
feel obliged to become Socialists also. Their representatives, indeed, conveyed the idea that they did
not view the Socialist programme without grave misapprehension. Thus, Mr. Maxwell, the chairman of
the Scottish Co-operative Wholesale Society, said :—
" Municipalities should be encouraged to undertake
the direction of productive industry only in those
spheres in which Co-operation has failed or cannot
hope to succeed. · No political authority ought to
compete against or to supplant voluntary co-operative
effort." [2] Mr. Mitchell, also, of the English Wholesale
Society, said :—" There would be no objection to
municipal bodies being empowered by law to supple-

[1] W. Min. 2375.

[2] W. Min. 654-62, 933-8.

ment the efforts made by co-operators towards the
democratic control of industry ; but it should be to
supplement—not to supplant—those efforts." [1] But,
whatever their apprehensions, it was clear from the
evidence that alliance rather than antagonism with
the Socialists was the accepted policy of the co-operative societies.   As Mr. Maxwell pointed out, the industrial enterprises of the State partake of the nature
of co-operative organisations in so far as they are representative of the people,[2] and the share which
Socialist bodies have had in building up the co-operative movement in the past is a matter of history.

The evidence taken before the Commission does not
enable us to extend our field of view to all the constituent movements of which the general movement
of labour is composed.   But enough has been said to
illustrate the accommodating spirit which marks the
relations of English Labour Movements to one another, and which to some extent justifies us in treating
them as a single united whole.   Of these, Socialism is
really a literary movement, and Co-operation does not
exist in view of the relation of employer and employed.   But even where exclusively Trade Unionist in
form, the Labour Movement is not exclusively Trade
Unionist in spirit.   Its policy is dictated by the will
of its adherents, who have learnt from Socialism to
widen their sympathies beyond the narrow boundaries
which Trade Unionism prescribes, and from Co-operation to look at industrial problems from the stand-
point of the capitalists whom Trade Unionism enables

[1] W. 356-405.
[2] W. Min. 654-62, 933-8.

them to fight. The Labour Movement, in short, is a complex, genuine, human force, at once too vigorous to perish and too strong to be crushed. The problem, therefore, is to bring it into harmony with existing industrial conditions, and to turn it from the abuses of industrial warfare to the uses of industrial peace.

CHAPTER II.

Collective Bargaining the Essence of Trade Unionism—But un-
recognised by Law—Conditions necessary for working it—
How a Union obtains the support of the Men—How a
Union obtains the Recognition of the Employers—Cause of
Strikes—The "old" and "new" Trade Unionism—Cost of
Strikes—Legality of Strikes—Development, Organisation,
and Conduct of Strikes—Tactics of Unions—Picketing and
Legislation relating thereto—Collection of Subscriptions—
Extension of Strikes over larger Areas—Federation of
Unions—Tactics of Employers—Blacklisting—Introduction
and Organisation of Non-Unionists—Extension of Lock-
outs over Larger Areas—Eviction—How a Union retains the
Allegiance of its Members—Benefits, Funds, etc.—How a
Union retains the Recognition of the Employers—How
Collective Bargaining can supersede Strikes—Summary,

ACCORDING to Mr. Sidney Webb, the essence of Trade
Unionism is " collective bargaining."[1] The phrase is
excellent, expressing, as it does, the fundamental distinction between the external and the internal aspects
of the movement. Viewed internally, its policy is
" collectivism "; viewed externally, its policy is
" bargaining." While prohibiting its members from
fighting their own battles, a Trade Union serves to
focus their individual forces and to make them the

[1] W. Min. 4501.

11

basis for future negotiations with their common adversaries.

"Bargaining" is not a strong word. But, for the purpose of defining the essential and permanent characteristics of the Trade Union movement, it is quite strong enough. It is true that all Unions resort to strikes at some period of their history, and many of them would appear to have adopted a systematic policy of striking. But the representatives even of these assured the Commission that this policy was adopted only in order to pave the way for the policy of " collective bargaining," which was at present impossible. " I hate strikes almost as much as I hate wars," said Mr. Price, the secretary of the Spike Nail-makers' Association.[1] And there is no reason to doubt that the declaration was sincere.

Yet, it will be said, strikes often take place, not only with the sanction, but apparently at the instigation of the Trade Union officials. Very often, indeed, the men seem individually inclined to settle their differences peacefully with their employers, when the " agitators " at the head of their organisations deliber- ately interrupt the " bargaining " which they profess to encourage, and insist upon substituting the policy of striking which they profess to abhor. Can it, therefore, be pretended that professions are sincere which are so flatly contradicted by practice ?

The fact cannot be disputed ; but it does not vitiate Mr. Webb's definition. The object for which a Trade Union is willing to order a strike is to realise, not " bargaining," but " *collective* bargaining." And

[1] A, II. Min. 17666.

this object is frustrated just as much when the men refuse to bargain collectively as when the employers refuse to bargain at all.

Now, "collective bargaining," as between employer and employed, is absolutely ignored by the law. Even in this the Trade Unions have gained one great point, for some years ago it was recognised as positively illegal on the ground that it was in restraint of trade. But, though no longer a crime, it is very far from being admitted to be a normal incident of a contract of service. On the contrary, an employer is regarded as having a separate and an independent contract with each one of his workmen, and every one of these contracts can be terminated only by a separate and an independent transaction. The men are allowed to strike collectively, but, before doing so, they must individually send in their notices.

This complete want of a legal *locus standi* in dealing with employers on behalf of their workmen, hampers a Trade Union at every stage of its career. If it stands firm, the employers can repudiate its interference, while, if it is prepared to make concessions, its own members can refuse to fulfil the promises it has made in their name. Before, therefore, it can realise its policy of " collective bargaining," it must solve the twofold problem—how to bind its own constituents, and how to obtain the recognition of the employers.

Of these problems, the first is infinitely more difficult than the second. And for this reason, that it must be solved before the second can even be approached. As the employers pointed out, it is not that they will not, but that they cannot recognise a weak Union, or conduct negotiations with delegates who cannot guarantee that their constituents will endorse the treaty.

Now, the origin of a Trade Union's power over its members is obviously a moral one. The infant organisation has no funds, and consequently no benefits to offer. It can, therefore, only come into being through the men's willingness to make some immediate personal sacrifice for their future collective benefit, and through their conviction that the Union will turn the sacrifices it asks them to make to good account. And in order to establish this conviction, which is the ultimate source of all its strength, the Union must show how strong it is already. Or rather, in order to acquire the moral support, which is to give it material power, it must, at the outset, prove itself to be possessed of capability and courage. It must, therefore, approach the employers with definite and reasonable requests, and a steady determination not to take "no!" for an answer.

If a Union acts thus, it will at once gain the confidence of the workmen. And if, in addition to this, it convinces the employers that it has gained that confidence, the battle is already half won. The evidence taken before the Commission shows that employers seldom fight or care to fight against an organisation which they feel really has the unqualified support of its members. Unfortunately, however, they often — and sometimes on good grounds—refuse to believe that the demands addressed to them by the Union officials are genuinely authorised by the workmen, and many of the representatives of the Unions complained that employers would not believe the men supported them until they had actually sent in their notices. In these circumstances, industrial warfare is not merely justifiable but necessary, if a Union is not to stultify itself at the critical stage of its career when it has to prove its right to existence in order that it may live.

Hence strikes, and hence, too, the reason why the weaker and the younger the Union, the more strikes is it bound to declare. And here let us take occasion to point out a very common error. Because a policy of striking is a temporary necessity of Unions that are young, it is often assumed to be a permanent characteristic of Unions that are modern; and it is argued that the tendency of industrial politics is, therefore, in the direction of war and not in the direction of peace. In other words, the difference in policy is attributed to a difference in principle instead of to a difference in circumstance. Never was there a greater fallacy. It is true that most of the Unions that have been formed in recent years are still obliged to spend a larger portion of their funds in strikes than their predecessors, that have already succeeded in making "collective bargaining" a reality; but this is not because they are modern, but merely because they are young. The representatives of the "new Unionists" informed the Commission that they desired industrial peace on the basis of "collective bargaining" fully as much as the old; but that, at present, they were unable to translate their desire into practice.

A policy of striking, then, may be said to be an in-

dication, not of a Union's principles, but of its progress. It is adopted, not from choice, but from
necessity. It is, however, a source of great evil. The
evidence abounds with narratives of the origin, development, and history of strikes, showing the great
hardships they inflict upon the strikers and the serious loss they occasion to the employers against whom
they are directed. From that evidence, one point, at
any rate, seems clear: that, though the loss to the
workmen is the more intense, the loss to the employers
is the more permanent. As was pointed out by Mr.
Giffen, the average duration of a strike does not
exceed three weeks, and the wages lost for so short a
time can, in most cases, be fully made up for by the
end of the year. "Indeed," he added, "the aggregate
direct loss in wages due to strikes does not amount to
one-fifth of one per cent. per annum; whereas the
loss inflicted upon the employers' businesses is much
more serious."[1] Of course, direct loss to the employers is indirect loss to the workmen; but Mr.
Giffen's statement points to an important conclusion
—that, in the conduct of industrial warfare, it is the
workmen who are generally the gainers by a truce.
And this conclusion is fully borne out by the facts
related by the witnesses. Very often the men return
to work after a strike, to all appearance thoroughly
beaten, and a few months afterwards persuade the
employers to grant their original demands without
any strike taking place at all.

When a strike occurs, the first question asked by
the public is, which party is in the right? Legally,

[1] W. Dig. p. 42.   Min. 6982-7.

the answer is, both. Provided that the proper notice is given, there is no breach of contract on either side. In fact, by the time the strike commences, there is no longer any contract to break. In the absence of express provision to the contrary, an ordinary contract of service is terminable by a month's notice, and what one man may do a thousand men may do also. At the beginning of the century, it is true, the Combination Acts expressly forbade a number of men from agreeing together to send in their notices on the same day; but, even then, a number of men might leave their employment *en masse*, provided that no such agreement or "conspiracy" existed, and now the Acts in question have been repealed. In fact, so long as the existing contract of hiring is legally terminated, a strike or a lock-out is perfectly legal, no matter how many men are affected, and how much damage is inflicted upon the trade of the country. The fact is so obvious and well known that we would not have insisted on it but for two purposes. First, to show that it abolishes the distinction between a strike and a lock-out. Of course, if there was a breach of contract, the distinction would be preserved. If an employer dismissed his men without giving them due notice, there would be a lock-out; while, if the men left their work without giving their employer due notice, there would be a strike. But where the contract has been legally terminated, and the quarrel simply resolves itself into a failure to come to terms concerning a new contract, the state of affairs may be described as either a strike or a lock-out, indifferently. Secondly, we have insisted on the legality of most

B

well-organised strikes, or lock-outs, because it is so often lost sight of in discussions on trade arbitration. But this is a matter which must be left over for the succeeding chapter.

The evidence relating to the development, organisation and conduct of strikes was peculiarly full and interesting. Broadly speaking, the methods pursued by the Trade Unions and the employers respectively, are four in number: by the former, picketing, collection of subscriptions, extension of the strike over a larger area, and federation; by the latter, blacklisting, introducing and organising non-unionists, extension of the lock-out over a larger area, and eviction.

Picketing consists in stationing men in the neighbourhood of a place where a strike is proceeding to inform the workmen of the fact. So long as it does consist in this, and nothing more, it is perfectly legal, no matter how many men are employed for the purpose. The Conspiracy and Protection of Property Act, however, while expressly declaring the legality of picketing for the purpose of giving information, renders liable to imprisonment or fine any person who *intimidates* or *persistently follows* any man proceeding to work or *besets* his house or place of work. The expressions italicised are not defined in the text, and the witnesses on each side were anxious to get this defect in the only Act directly affecting the conduct of industrial warfare remedied in their favour. Thus, the representatives of the Trade Unions desired the term " intimidation " to be defined so as to include such threats only as are accompanied by actual physical violence, or are calculated to put a man in reasonable bodily fear, although some of them preferred to make the definition sufficiently strict to cover the following actions on the part of the employers, *viz.*, blacklisting, eviction at less than three months' notice, dismissal without assignment of a valid reason, and the engagement of men during a strike without informing them of its existence. The employers' representatives all desired the definition to cover the moral intimidation exercised by the assemblage of more than three men in the neighbourhood of industrial establishments for the purpose of picketing, the right of giving information being confined to the right of holding public meetings, advertising in the newspapers, and canvassing the workmen's own homes. They also desired the penalties for offences under the Act to be increased, and to take the form of imprisonment in every case ; whereas the men desired cumulative penalties to be disallowed, and judges to be deprived of the power of withholding the option of a fine, except with the advice of a jury.

Collection of subscriptions from the public is an ordinary incident of every large strike. Sometimes, moreover, pickets are sent into the streets with moneyboxes to extort contributions from non-unionist workmen. Thus, Mr. W. Chapman, the chairman of the Metropolitan Cab Proprietors' Strike Fund Association, stated that this form of blackmailing was carried to such an extent that it was practically impossible for any London cabdriver to avoid subscribing to the Union funds during a strike, and he considered that the law should be strengthened in such a way as to make it illegal.[1]

[1] B. III. Min. 19115.

Extension of the strike over a larger area is a device frequently adopted when the balance of force seems to be against the strikers in a particular locality. It presupposes some sort of alliance between the various Unions connected with the same trade or district, and such alliance admits of various degrees, and may be either temporary or permanent. The general tendency is for the Unions to draw closer together, until they become permanently amalgamated. Thus, pressure from without has gradually welded together almost all the associations of engineers, and almost all the various associations connected with each of the other trades concerned with engineering and shipbuilding. And all these amalgamated Unions connected with the shipbuilding industry are in process of uniting under a common organisation, in spite of—and, in point of fact, to settle—their frequent mutual quarrels. A similar tendency is observable in the mining and other industries, and the valuable Blue Book on the Rules of Associations, published by the Royal Commission on Labour, affords ample material for tracing the steps by which the various Unions are passing from alliance to affiliation, from affiliation to federation, and from federation to amalgamation.

This development takes two different courses. It proceeds either from trade to trade or from district to district. Among the skilled workers, or old Unionists, the former course is the more usual ; among the unskilled or new Unionists, the latter is preferred. In fact, the only sound distinction of principle that can be drawn between the old Unionism and the new, is that the former is more particularly the Unionism of trades, whereas the latter is more often the Unionism of localities. This distinction is often apparent in the very titles of the Unions. Contrast, for example, the title "Amalgamated Society of Engineers" with the title "South Side Labour Protection League." In many cases, moreover, where the trade nomenclature is adopted by a new unionist organisation, membership is wholly unconnected with occupation. The Gas Workers' and General Labourers' Union, for example, has on its books representatives of no fewer than sixty-nine different trades,[1] even including textile workers; and the Dockers' Union embraces, or did at one time embrace, a considerable number of agricultural labourers.

Federation, whether by trades or by districts, is a great source of strength. Not only does it enable the strike area to be extended, but it often makes such extension unnecessary by enabling the accumulated funds of the wider organisation to be promptly placed at the disposal of the trade or district originally affected, and an employer might well hesitate before fighting single-handed with a body of men deriving an indefinite amount of financial support from persons whom the dispute in no way concerned. Indeed, it is the great extension of federation in recent years that has obliged the employers—always reluctant to join hands with their trade competitors—to themselves form associations on the lines of the men's Trade Unions for the purposes of mutual support. Without these associations, they would be unable, in a strike

[1] C. III. Min. 24535-40.

of large extent, to work the various devices available
to them on a sufficiently large scale.

Of these devices, the commonest is blacklisting, or the
agreement not to employ certain men, or bodies of
men, that have rendered themselves obnoxious to other
employers. According to the rules of Iron Trades'
Employers' Association and the Monmouthshire and
South Wales Coal Owners' Association, no member
may employ any workman from the workshops or
colliery of another member affected by a strike or
lock-out;[1] and the rules of the Lanarkshire Coal
Masters' Association forbid the members to engage
any new workman during a strike or lock-out at a
colliery belonging to one of their body or to a member
of a similar Association that guarantees reciprocal
action.[2]   In the Yorkshire Master Printers' and Allied
Trades' Association and the Leeds Boot Manufacturers'
Association, moreover, a list of the men on strike is
circulated amongst the members, and they are subject
to a fine if they employ any man whose name is on
the list.

The introduction and organisation of non-unionists is
not often expressly provided for in the rules of employers' associations; indeed, Rule 6 of the Liverpool
Employers' Labour Association, which provides that
"in the event of strikes seeming imminent, it is the
duty of the association to obtain an immediate supply
of outside labour, and to arrange accommodation and
police protection," seems to be unique in this respect.[3]

[1] See Blue Book on Rules of Associations, pp. 100, 106.
[2] *Id.*, p. 110.
[3] *Id.*, p. 144.

But, although not expressly provided for in the rules, the supply of non-unionist labour is well looked after, and often elaborately organised by the associations. This is notably the case with the Shipping Federation, which offers preference of employment to all seamen that are furnished with tickets of membership in the Free Labour Association started in opposition to the National Amalgamated Sailors' and Firemen's Union. Mr. J. Havelock Wilson pointed out that such organisations were not really "free," for they were managed by and in the interests of persons who were not members.[1] It is certain that they serve to greatly strengthen the position of the employers. Not only do they render the supply of non-unionist labour more easily available in case of strikes, but they tend to insure employers against strikes altogether. They attract the men that might otherwise join the Unions, and, having once secured their patronage, find an effective guarantee for their future good behaviour in the entrance fees and subscriptions.

Extension of the lock-out over a larger area sometimes finds favour with the employers' associations in order to protect individual members that are engaged in a struggle with the Unions. A good instance of this is afforded in the evidence of Mr. Glennie, the secretary of the Tyneside district section of the Amalgamated Society of Engineers, who said:—"In the beginning of 1891, when the engineers employed in Messrs. Palmers' yard at Jarrow struck because the agreed upon demarcation of work between themselves and the plumbers was not respected, all the employers in

[1] B. I. Min. 9335.

the Wear and Tyne district locked out all the members of the Engineers' Society in their service."[1] It
is noticeable that both employers and employed in
this industry seem to recognise that the practice of
extending strikes and lock-outs over larger areas has its
disadvantages, for Captain Noble, the chairman of the
Tyne and Wear district section of the Iron Trades
Employers' Association, stated that an agreement—
too frequently broken—had been made to the effect
that no part in a dispute affecting the Tyne and Wear
district should be taken by members of either side
beyond that area.[2]

The last device adopted by employers to combat
strikes is eviction. This, of course, can only be resorted to where the employers are also the landlords
of their workpeople, and, in urban industries, such is
not generally the case. In the Scotch mining districts,
however, eviction is a not unfrequent incident of
important strikes ; indeed, the houses are occupied on
tenure of employment, so that eviction accompanies a
strike as a matter of course. The Trade Unions considered that the law should refuse to recognise such
a tenure, and, wherever possible, they encouraged
their members to reside off the employers' estates.

Having, then, very briefly reviewed the methods
ordinarily adopted during a strike, let us resume the
thread of our argument at the point where we broke
it off. It was seen that, in the first stage of a Trade
Union's history, strikes were necessary in order to
convince the employers that it really had the support

[1] A. III. Min. 23080-99.
[2] A. III. Min. 25203-4.

of its members. Let us suppose that it has triumph-
antly passed through the ordeal. That, after a strike
of several months' duration, the members are still
loyal to the organisation for whose sake they have
endured such great suffering, and that terms of
peace have been arranged by the "collective bargaining," which the employers had at first so indignantly
repudiated. Should we be justified in expecting that,
so far as that Union was concerned, the era of strikes
was past? By no means. Before "collective bargaining" can become a settled habit, other conditions must be fulfilled.

In the first place, the Union must prove that it can
reckon upon the same loyalty on the part of its members in time of peace as it has received in time of war.
And this even the strongest of Unions can hardly be
said to do. The evidence is full of instances where
men, that have endured the miseries of a strike for
weeks and even months at a time without a murmur
and in perfect obedience to their officials, yet, on the
most trivial grounds, refuse to endorse the terms which
those officials have arranged with the employers. It
is to combat this great and omnipresent difficulty
that many of the Unions make very strict rules against
members leaving their employment without the sanction of the executive, the offence being in the case of
the Tyneside and National Labour Union punishable
by expulsion.[1] But, even where such rules exist, the
Unions do not always dare to enforce them. Thus,
the Amalgamated Society of Carpenters and Joiners
recently supported a strike undertaken in defiance of

[1] See Blue Book on Rules of Associations, p. 115.

its authority by some of its members employed in the shipbuilding trade at Newcastle. And, even if such rules are enforced, they do nothing to prevent a section of the members, dissatisfied with an agreement made by the executive on their behalf, from dissociating themselves from the Union *en masse.* Thus, the enginemen and cranemen left the Blastfurnacemen's Association and set up an independent organisation of their own, directly the operation of the sliding scale, drawn up with the consent of their representatives, began to cause a reduction in their wages.[1] As was pointed out by Mr. H. Bell, the employers' representative, it would be impossible to bargain with the Unions if this sort of thing happened often, for one cannot negotiate with a body that one cannot grasp.[2]

One of the most interesting features of industrial politics is the way in which Trade Unions gradually contrive to make their hold over their members effective. The most common device is to create a fund for the purpose of providing Friendly Society benefits, and so to give each member a direct personal interest in keeping up his connection with the organisation. The success of this policy is evidenced by the fact that the Unions that give the most benefits of this kind are at once the strongest and the best able to command the confidence of the employers.

Some of the larger societies supplement their policy in this respect by giving a central executive council full and absolute control over all the funds collected through its various branches. The evidence of Mr. R.

---

[1] A. II. Min. 14528-31, 14610, 14648.
[2] *Id.*

Knight, the general secretary of the Boilermakers' and Iron Shipbuilders' Society, is instructive on this point. He said:—" The administration of the affairs of the Union is vested in an executive council composed of seven members, each of whom is elected by one of the branches established within a certain area. As a guarantee that the Union funds shall not be spent in unnecessary disputes, the members of the executive council have full control over them. In no case can one penny be spent in a dispute without their sanction, and, before granting it, they make every effort, generally with success, to get the difficulty adjusted peaceably. Even if a strike proves inevitable, and does occur with their sanction, they have power to declare it settled, if they consider the terms offered by the employers to be acceptable. Subject, moreover, to the control of the council which holds the purse strings, local disputes are also adjusted by the district agents of the Union. The council firmly exercises its strong powers over the members of the Union, and they in their turn loyally obey it, since they themselves have moulded its policy by making the rules which it carries into effect. Notwithstanding the fact that its members continue to practise the trade which it represents, the council claims to be as impartial as it is powerful. For it represents the Union as a whole, and not any of the individual districts that successive disputes may affect. It does not conduct the meetings of the men concerned in a dispute, but simply deals with any business that may be sent to its office. Recognising the ultimate community of interest between labour and capital, the council is guided in its actions by the interest of the trade as a whole. It does not hold a brief for one side. Its independent character has enabled it to be a specially beneficial means of controlling disputes." [1]

Besides the arrangements made by the Unions themselves for protecting their funds against their members, the legislature has, whether intentionally or not, strengthened their hands considerably by inserting in the Trade Union Act, 1871, a clause to the effect that "nothing in this Act shall enable any court to entertain any legal proceedings instituted with the object of directly enforcing or recovering damages for the breach of any agreement for the application of the funds of a Trade Union to provide benefits to members." The result is that a Union can stop the payment of benefits at any moment by merely altering the rules that constitute the sole guarantee that such payment will be made. Many societies, moreover, have taken the precaution of providing in advance for the suspension of benefits when the funds fall below a certain figure, thereby escaping the necessity of amending the rules in times of emergency.

Finally, the hold of the Unions over their members is greatly strengthened by the mere fact of expansion. When a Society acquires a practical monopoly of its trade, as the boilermakers' has almost succeeded in doing, and, as is generally the case, forbids its members to work with non-unionists, resignation of membership necessarily involves loss of employment.

[1] A. III. Dig. 21. Min. 20683-97, 20713-8, 20946-50, 20976-8, 21011-27.

To acquire such monopoly, therefore, and, having acquired it, to keep it, is a cardinal point in the policy of every Trade Union.

Now, even if a Union does succeed in making its hold over its members for all practical purposes complete, and in convincing the employers of its strength for both war and peace alike, it will never retain "recognition" so long as its attitude is one of unreasoning hostility. As Mr. Livesey pointed out, there can be no bargaining with a body whose watchword is simply, " Give us all we ask," for the person so addressed will naturally feel that concession will be only the prelude to further demands.[1] A Union must not only show its power, but it must at the same time show that peace is possible and expedient Even the most combative of Trade Unions recognise this truth at a very early stage of their career. Thus, the National Amalgamated Sailors' and Firemen's Union declares one of its objects to be " to provide a better class of men for the merchant service, and to see that all members that are engaged through the Union be on board at the appointed time,.and in a sober condition ready for work," and, immediately upon its formation, in 1887, its secretary drew up a circular letter to the shipowners, asking for their cooperation and sympathy.[2] The majority of the Unions, moreover, have rules enjoining upon their members courteousness of demeanour and propriety of behaviour towards their employers.

Provided that a Union be strong, and provided that

[1] C. III. Dig. p. 44.
[2] B. I. Min. 9241-6, 9705-6.

it associates its courage to fight with a sincere desire for industrial peace, it seldom has much difficulty in securing the recognition of the employers. Several of the representatives of the latter examined before the Commission declared that they found it better to deal with a responsible executive than with an "unorganised mass." Obviously so, we may fairly exclaim, seeing that it is with the "responsible executive" that the decision really rests. Indeed, it seems as foolish for an employer to negotiate with individuals after they have surrendered the determination of the issue to the officials of their Union, as it would be for a Government to accredit an ambassador to a monarch that had abdicated.

But, however willing an employer may be to come to terms with a Union, he does not always dare to do so. In the present stress of competition, one firm cannot make concessions independently of its rivals without bankruptcy staring it in the face. Before, therefore, "collective bargaining" can work, it is necessary for the employers to be as well organised as the men. And this is scarcely ever the case. The evidence abounds in complaints made by the men's representatives of the inability of the employers' associations to bind their members. Thus, Mr. Cronin, the general secretary of the Associated Society of the Millmen of Scotland, stated that the first employer to defy the authority of a newly established wages board was none other than the chairman himself, and that his example was faithfully followed by his successor in the office ![1]

[1] A. II. Min. 15938-64, 15985-16114, 16234-8, 16316.

This weakness can be overcome only by the action of the men. As was pointed out by Mr. Allan, the head of a firm of marine engineers, the interests of the members of an employers' association are essentially competing, and can be forced into co-operation only by pressure from without.[1] It is the policy of the Unions, therefore, to extend the operation of arrangements made between themselves and the employers that happen to recognise them to every firm in which their members are employed, with the result that recusant employers have to choose between acting in concert with their fellows and losing all voice in the determination of the contracts which they will have to make with their own workmen. By this means, the employers' organisations become, not only equally strong with those of the men, but, what is just as important, equally extensive, and it is then, and not till then, that "collective bargaining" can become the ordinary method of deciding the questions that arise between employers and employed.

To sum up—the essence of Trade Unionism is "collective bargaining," and "collective bargaining" is made possible when the rival organisations of employers and employed, being imbued with a desire for industrial peace, survive the hostilities they originally came into existence to conduct, and provide their representatives with definite homogeneous constituencies.

[1] W. Min. 6832-9.

CHAPTER III.

CONCILIATION AND ARBITRATION.

Methods of Compromise—Conciliation defined—Under what circumstances is it successful ?—Is it an appropriate Function of Government?—Arbitration defined — Why Compulsory Arbitration is at present impossible—Voluntary Arbitration—Qualifications essential to a successful Arbitrator—A possible Solution of the Labour Question—Legal Position of Trade Unions—Its bearing on Arbitration— Natural Development of Trade Arbitration—Its History, 1800-1894—Summary of Arguments—Industrial Policies of Socialists, Trade Unions, and Workmen—How they are related.

IT may, then, be confidently asserted that the only means of avoiding strikes is either to crush Trade Unionism or to perfect the machinery for working "collective bargaining." At the same time, it is hardly necessary to point out that the most severe strikes are due to failure to work the perfected machinery successfully. The members of a joint board, clothed with adequate authority, imbued with a desire for industrial peace, and representing definite homogeneous constituencies, may, and often do, honestly fail to come to terms, or to convince one another of the justice of their respective claims. Such a situation admits of only two solutions—warfare or compromise, and it is with methods of compromise that it is now proposed to deal.

It was pointed out by Mr. Taylor, of the Gas Workers' Union, that no amount of argument would ever persuade an employer that he ought to pay 7d. an hour, when he thought he ought only to pay 6½d.[1] This is undoubtedly the case; but it is equally true to say that an employer would often concede a demand, which he considered excessive, rather than face a strike, which would be rendered all the more formidable from the perfection of the organisation designed to make strikes unnecessary. The fear of strikes would influence the men in the same peaceable direction. It is not surprising, therefore, to find that, in the most highly organised trades, compromise is common, while strikes are comparatively rare.

Compromise, however, is never accepted without reluctance, and never suggested without greater reluctance still. Each party waits for the other to make the first concession, with the result that negotiation is often prematurely suspended—much to the vexation of both.

In such cases, the intervention of a third party to suggest the compromise which is to form the basis of future discussion is very welcome. This form of intervention may be called conciliation, in contradistinction to arbitration, which will be described hereafter. It can take place either before or after the suspension of negotiations has resulted in a strike. The action of Lord Rosebery in regard to the coal strike of 1893,

[1] C. III. Min. 23477-89.

C

is a noteworthy example of conciliation, which will at once occur to the reader. It will be remembered, moreover, that the Durham coal strike of the previous year was brought to a close in a similar manner, through the intervention of the Bishop of the diocese.[1]

So much good has resulted from the kindly intervention of third parties in this way, that several witnesses—notably, Mr. Tom Mann—desired a permanent Board of Conciliation to be established in connection with the new Labour Department. This Board, Mr. Mann suggested, should be composed of six persons, elected by the Trade Unions, and six by the Associations of Employers, with an official of the Department to act as president. In order to encourage settlement between the parties as much as possible, the Board should not be authorised to interfere until hostilities had lasted a fortnight, but it should then investigate the matter on its own responsibility, publish the facts and issue a recommendation as to the basis of compromise, trusting to public opinion to secure the recommendation being carried into effect.[2]

With regard to this and all similar proposals, it must be remembered that conciliation cannot succeed unless there is a willingness on the part of employers and workmen to compromise the matter in dispute. A recommendation that neither party would accept would only tend to complicate the quarrel it was intended to solve. Success, moreover, amounts to no more than the reopening of negotiation. The ultimate

[1] A. III. Dig. pp. 8-10.
[2] W. Min. 2752-81, 3320-6, 3441-75, 3551-65.

decision still rests with the joint boards, and their success depends upon the fulfilment of the various conditions enumerated in the preceding chapter. The field for conciliation is, accordingly, very much narrowed, and the conciliating individual or board must exercise the most careful discretion before deciding to intervene.

It was for this reason, among others, that Dr. Gould, one of the statistical experts in the United States Labour Department, objected to conciliation in trade disputes becoming one of the recognised functions of Government. His view was that the head of a department engaged in collecting accurate information concerning the conditions of labour, might usefully intervene unofficially, for he would then be able to exercise his own discretion and mediate at the right time, in the right place, and in the right manner. But to make conciliation part of the regular official duties in respect of which a body of public servants were paid, Dr. Gould considered to be out of the question, for they would either enjoy the privilege of being idle at discretion, or would make confusion worse confounded by ill-timed meddling.[1]

Again, suppose a sub-department of conciliation were attached to the Board of Trade, the minister at the head of that department would be perpetually bullied by his political friends and foes to mediate prematurely, and, if he yielded to the pressure, would only offend both the disputants, and very likely cause them to prolong the fight out of sheer obstinacy.[2]

[1] W. Min. 6517-26, 6566, 6749-82.

[2] *Id.*

In short, it may be laid down as an axiom that conciliation which does not lead back to "collective bargaining" is a failure, and it is, therefore, in their relation to "collective bargaining" that all proposed schemes of conciliation must be judged.

Conciliation and arbitration must be carefully distinguished. They are different in origin, nature, and result. Whereas conciliation originates when negotiation is suspended, consists in the intervention of a third party on his own initiative to suggest a basis of compromise, and results in negotiation being resumed, arbitration originates when negotiation is proceeding, consists in the reference of the issue to a third party, and results in the matter being decided.

Where negotiation is suspended, there arbitration cannot arise. The parties must negotiate in order to settle who the arbitrator is to be, and what are to be the terms of reference. Otherwise a third party could have no authority to take the decision out of their hands. Several witnesses, indeed, desired the requisite authority to be given by Parliament. But, as was pointed out in the preceding chapter, the relation of employer and employed ceases with the contract that created it. The legislature, therefore, must declare the relation of employer and employed to exist independently of contract before it can give an arbitrator authority to interpret the rights and duties which, independently of contract, the relation implies. It is absurd to create machinery for the administration of a body of law that does not exist. Yet this is what most of the proposals for compulsory State arbitration concerning the terms of future contracts really involve.

Arbitration, then, can arise only from the voluntary action of a joint board. Before it can work, moreover, not only must all the conditions essential to "collective bargaining" be present, but they must be present in a superlative degree. It does not at all follow that, because individuals are willing to allow a joint board to settle the terms of their contracts, they will allow it to delegate its authority to an irresponsible third party. It is of paramount importance, therefore, that the arbitrator should enjoy the confidence, not only of the members, but also of the constituents of the board from which he derives his authority.

Where organisation is really strong, the members of the boards are sometimes invested with authority to submit any question to arbitration they may think fit, and their constituents are pledged to endorse the appointment and accept the award. In most cases, however, the members are obliged to consult their constituents by ballot before taking such a step, and it is probable that the agents of even the strongest organisations would hesitate before consenting to refer an important question to an arbitrator whose name was not known and respected by their principals.

Now, what is the sort of man whose name is likely to be known and respected? In the first place, a man occupying a distinguished position in virtue of his connection with the trade or district where the dispute occurs. Such are mayors of towns, lords lieutenant of counties, members of Parliament, employers of labour, and leading Trade Union representatives— from all which classes the evidence showed that arbitrators were frequently selected. In the second place, arbitrators are often looked for among distinguished men whose want of local and technical knowledge is regarded as a proof of disinterestedness. Such are the bishops and clergy, and judges, barristers and other members of the legal profession. But with all these classes of persons to choose from, the witnesses complained that satisfactory arbitrators were rare. The mayors, members of Parliament, employers and Trade Unionists, they said, were seldom disinterested; and the clergy, barristers and judges did not understand the " technicalities " of the trade or the wants of the district. In other words, the former did not know how to pronounce fair judgments upon the body of fact and sentiment which they understood, and the latter did not understand the body of fact and sentiment upon which they were asked to adjudicate.

Disinterestedness and sympathy, then, are both indispensable qualities for a successful arbitrator. The fact of the appointment being made by Government from the ranks of the legal profession, might guarantee disinterestedness, but could never guarantee sympathy, and, for this reason, many of the witnesses were not disposed to recommend the establishment of State Arbitration Boards, even without compulsory power. Everything, they considered, would depend upon their *personnel.* One successful appointment would not guarantee the success of future appointments. And there is no reason to suppose that Government would find it easier to discover men of the right stamp than the parties themselves.

Satisfactory arbitrators are very scarce, but, happily, not undiscoverable. The success of arbitration in the pottery trade was attributed by the witnesses to the personal qualities of the man to whom the cases were invariably referred—a man who combined perfect disinterestedness with an adequate knowledge of the "technicalities" (*i.e.*, the etiquette, traditions and customs) of the trade, and a large experience of former verdicts.[1]

It is by studying the methods and decisions of such men, as well as those of the joint boards themselves and the results of strikes, that a solution of the labour question might possibly be found. As was pointed out above, the main obstacle to compulsory State arbitration is the absence of a body of law on which decisions could be based; but it is conceivable that the State might be able to find in the recorded issues of former disputes the body of law required. Mr. Parry, of the North Wales Quarrymen's Union, suggested that Parliament should enact a code of laws to guide arbitrators in making their awards.[2] In the records of the past there might be found a code of laws ready to hand, if somebody would only take the trouble to formulate it.

The legal enforcement of awards based upon precedents voluntarily created might not be impossible. The success of the Associated Iron and Steel Workers' Union in compelling its members to abide by awards, is largely due to the fact that the arbitrator—to quote the evidence of Mr. Whitwell—" is guided by certain

[1] C. III. Min. 30382-401.
[2] A. II. Min. 9615-8.

settled rules, supplemented by his own common sense."[1] No doubt it is very difficult to deduce any " settled rules " from a number of decisions that seem to rest almost exclusively upon minute questions of fact; but the establishment and working of sliding scales, which consist in the discovery of a settled rule to govern the decision of the largest group of contentious questions (*i.e.*, questions of wages) in advance, proves that it is sometimes possible to do so.

At all events, it is conceivable that much good might result if the Government were to place at the disposal of arbitrators, voluntarily chosen, a permanent clerical staff to chronicle the process and result of their work. Such a staff, being paid by the Treasury, would save the parties a great deal of expense, would enable arbitrations to be conducted on a systematic and uniform plan, and would be the means of transmitting to its successive chiefs the experience of their predecessors. Thus, from respecting the person of the arbitrator, disputants would in time come to respect the office.

Instead, however, of seeking to extend the application of accepted decisions to future cases, most of the proposals made by the witnesses aimed rather at getting unacceptable decisions enforced. To this end, the most important proposal was to incorporate the Trade Unions, or, at any rate, to give them sufficient legal personality to enable the members of joint boards to deposit a substantial sum out of the funds of their constituent organisations as a guarantee that arbitrators' awards would be accepted. At present, a

[1] A. II. Min. 15010-6, 15037-8.

Trade Union has no legal existence apart from its
constituent members, individuals do not lose their
proprietorship in the collective fund, and disburse-
ments from that fund, or promises to disburse, can be
made only in so far as is expressly authorised by the
rules under which the members consented to pay
their subscriptions.   On general grounds, therefore,
the proposed incorporation of Trade Unions has much
to recommend it from the Trade Unionist point of
view ; but, considered in its relation to arbitration, it
seems to call for some comment.   In the first place,
it will be observed that the officials of an incorporated Union, though able to hypothecate the corporate
funds, would not be compelled to do so, and the
experience of the past conclusively proves that they
would not do so voluntarily.   Legislation providing
special facilities for arbitration on condition that the
parties consent to bind themselves in some way to
obey it, already exists; but disputants have never yet
been induced to sign the contracts necessary to bring
it into operation.   Again, it would be most unbusiness-
like for a corporation to make itself legally responsible for the actions of individuals over whom it had
no legal control.   Individuals would still enjoy perfect freedom to renew or refuse to renew contracts of
service on the terms laid down by the arbitrator.   As
was pointed out by . Mr. Freak, representing the
National Union of Boot and Shoe Operatives, the
effect of pledging the corporate funds " would simply
be punishing the good man for the bad, for the fine
would come out of the pockets of those who remained
members ; whereas those who wished to repudiate the

award, and, therefore, deserted the Union, would carry on their blacklegging and bear no penalty at all, and no arrangement could be made to prevent individual members leaving their Union in contempt of an award."[1] Of course, it may be said that the Union need only pledge itself not to sanction or support strikes undertaken by rebellious members against awards. Several witnesses, however, including Mr. Boulton of the London Chamber of Commerce, warned the Commission that the members would not endorse any such undertaking.[2] The policy of a Union must depend upon the vote of the majority of the members. Of course, where the persons repudiating the award were a small portion of the members, the central executive would be able to restrain them. But the executive could only act thus when it had a majority of the members at its back, and, in these cases, the deposit of a guarantee would be superfluous. In fact, the hypothecation of a Union's funds would have no binding force at all. At most, it would be a bet that the Union officials would receive the voluntary support of the members in a particular instance. Where they had such support, the bet would be unnecessary, and, where they had not, the bet would never be made. One thing, therefore, seems clear, that so long as it is individuals who contract to serve, it is impossible to bind corporations not to strike.

Arbitration in trade disputes must be suffered to develop. It cannot be manufactured, and its growth cannot be forced. How rapid and consistent that

[1] C. III. Min. 33208-9.
[2] W. Min. 4996-5019.

growth is naturally, the secretary to the Commission clearly shows in his memorandum on the Rules of Associations. "The history of conciliation and arbitration in England," he writes, "may be divided into three periods, each possessing certain distinctive characteristics. The first period ends in 1860, before which date industrial tendencies and public opinion had for many years been setting towards the adoption of some equitable and amicable method of settling disputes relating to wages and other industrial conditions. This found expression . . . . in the establishment of various voluntarily created boards of conciliation or courts of arbitration in connection with different industries, of which some were temporarily successful, but none of a thoroughly systematic or permanent character. The second period ends in 1889. It is marked by the transition of the system of conciliation and arbitration from an experimental stage to one of full development and efficiency, the years 1860 to 1880 being occupied in an almost unbroken series with the establishment of voluntary boards of arbitration and conciliation in the most important of the English industries. These all enjoyed a more or less prolonged success, which, in several cases, has lasted to the present day. The third period, from 1889 onwards, has seen the introduction and development of an entirely new phase in the history of arbitration and conciliation, *viz.*, the establishment of local boards of arbitration and conciliation, generally in connection with the Chamber of Commerce and Trades Council in the district to which they belong, which are not restricted in action to one industry, but intended to settle disputes arising in any local trade."

With reference to the first period, the secretary proceeds to point out that the first trade to adopt arbitration appears to have been the printers', and that disputes in the pottery trade have invariably been settled by arbitration since 1836, although no permanent board was established in that industry till 1868.

Of the permanent boards established in the second period, perhaps the most important is the Board of Arbitration and Conciliation for the Manufactured Iron and Steel Trade of the North of England, which has practically succeeded in banishing strikes from the industry. This is specially noticeable, because, up to the time of its establishment in 1869, in no trade had strikes been more frequent, disastrous and prolonged. Of late years the number of cases coming before it has tended to decrease; but that is not because the men have preferred to strike, but partly because the trade itself has diminished in extent, and chiefly because successive arbitrations have finally established a sufficient number of points to materially diminish the occasions of dispute.[1]

The territorial character of the boards established since 1889, of which the London Labour Conciliation Board is a typical example,[2] may perhaps be connected with the territorial character of the new Unionism referred to in the preceding chapter. Where the men are organised on territorial lines, the employers must

[1] A. II. Dig. pp. 44-46.
[2] W. Dig. pp. 31, 32.

organise on territorial lines also, and the sphere of the joint boards necessarily coincides with that of its constituent organisations.

The secretary's account of the growth of boards of conciliation and arbitration is really an account of the development of what Mr. Sidney Webb called " collective bargaining." These Boards are not composed of conciliators and arbitrators, but of representatives of the disputants. Inasmuch, however, as they all make provision in their rules for the reference to arbitration of cases they cannot decide, and inasmuch as arbitration is impossible without them, their history and the history of trade arbitration are practically identical.

To sum up : compulsory State arbitration, in the absence of a body of law on which to base decisions, is impossible ; voluntary State arbitration, which did not base its awards upon a knowledge of the traditions and customs of trade and district, would not be accepted ; and an Act enabling the awards of voluntarily-appointed arbitrators to be enforced against the Union funds would be inoperative. But it might be possible to extract from a systematic record of the work of voluntary Boards, a body of acceptable law, which the State might some day administer and enforce.

With the development and working of methods of " collective bargaining," conciliation and arbitration, the work of Trade Unionism ceases. And it is at this point that the Socialists take up their parable. " Look," they say, " how inefficient a force this Trade Unionism is. It can only get its machinery to work successfully in a set of peculiarly favourable conditions —conditions, which are to be created only by dint of protracted warfare, involving terrible suffering to the combatants and permanent damage to trade, and which, when created, are ever liable to disappear when trade is bad and funds are low. And when the machinery does work, "collective bargaining," conciliation and arbitration are the meagre result. Why should the workman stoop to "bargain" now that he is the chief power in the State, and can command? If he wants more wages and less work, let him simply promote an Act of Parliament to say that he is to have them."

The argument is attractive, but by no means unanswerable. Assuming that Parliament is omnipotent, and that " the workman's " control over it is absolute and complete, it no more follows that the members of any given trade will get Acts of Parliament to suit them, than the abolition of human slavery follows from man's lordship over creation. As a matter of fact, " the workman " can only with the greatest difficulty be persuaded to entrust the settlement of questions that immediately concern his interests to a Trade Union, of which he forms perhaps the one-thousandth part. Much less is he inclined to entrust it to the British Parliament, of which he represents a still smaller fraction of a single member. He allows the Trade Union to do for him only what he is not strong enough to do for himself; and, on the same principle, he will allow Parliament to act only when the Trade Union has failed. The corporate policy of the Unions is the same. They do not want the State to help them where they are able to help themselves ; and, in spite of Mr. Keir Hardie's assurance to the contrary,[1] the evidence clearly showed that strong State Socialism and weak Trade Unionism always went together.[2] Some Unions object to State interference so strongly that they are unwilling to invoke its aid even when they seem to need it. A remarkable instance of this is afforded by the Associated Iron and Steel Workers' Union. In this case, the Union officials want to establish an eight hours' working day. The employers are willing to grant it. But the men themselves insist on working longer hours. Yet, when Mr. Trow was asked whether he would approve of the hours being fixed by Parliament, he absolutely repudiated the suggestion. " The Trade Union officials," he said, " know more about the wants of their own members in their own districts than all the members of Parliament."[3]

Socialistic, in fact, as the labour movement is, it is undoubtedly individualistic as well. Individuals and organisations may need help, but they do not want their own exertions to be made unnecessary. In the following chapters, it is proposed to take each of the conditions of labour in turn, and, in the case of each, the reader will be able to note what force the workman means to use in order to secure their improvement—how far he will trust to himself, how far to his Union, and how far to the State ; and, as a general result, it will be found that his policy is determined by the principles laid down in the preceding paragraph.

[1] A. II. Min. 13163-72.
[2] A. II. Min. 13567.
[3] A. II. Min. 15242-3.

PART II.

CONDITIONS OF LABOUR.

CHAPTER I.

INDUSTRIAL REMUNERATION.

Wages Statistics—Should Government fix Rates of Wages ?—
Government as a Wage Payer—The Law relating to
Methods of Payment—The Truck Acts—Payment of Wages
out of a Bankrupt's Estate—The Payment of wages in Public
Houses Prohibition Act—Sliding Scales—Definition and
working of—Presuppose Organisation—Advantages of—
Difficulties in working—Effect of, on Trade Unions —
How far can they be permanent ?—Profit-sharing—Defini-
tion and working of—Profit-sharing does not involve Loss-
sharing—Profit-sharing and Wage-earning—Its working
under the South Metropolitan Gas Company—Attitude of
Trade Unions towards Profit-sharing—And towards all
Methods of Payment by results.

IT would be useless to attempt to include in a short
work of this kind a statement of the wages paid to
all the different classes of workers represented before
the Commission. Suffice it to say, that the variety in
the earnings of manual labourers is enormous, ranging,
as it does, from the £10 or £12 a week, which, Mr. Trow
said, was made by the best paid of the members of the

Associated Iron and Steel Workers' Union,[1] to the mere "keep" which, according to Mr. C. Booth, was the only remuneration given to some of the workers in the East End of London.[2]

Mr. Giffen put in evidence some interesting figures, showing the average annual income of the adult male labourer to be £60, and of labourers of every age and sex £48, and stated that, of a total national income of about £1,500,000,000, about £633,000,000 was appropriated to the manual labourers in the form of wages, as against £867,000,000 appropriated otherwise.[3] But he pointed out that these statistics did not afford the information, which, at first sight, they might appear to afford, as to the relation between profits and wages, for the three following reasons:—

(*a*) That a very large portion of the £867,000,000 represents wages, though not the wages of manual labour.

(*b*) That another very large portion of the £867,000,000 represents the interest on English capital invested abroad, whereas the £633,000,000 does not include the wages of the foreign labour it employs.

(*c*) That the figures are inevitably inaccurate owing to the difficulty of determining, in the case of a great deal of income, what portion of it is of the nature of wages, what of the nature of profit, and what of the nature of interest.[4]

[1] A. II. Dig. p. 46 ; Min. 15166, 15287-300.
[2] W. Dig. p 26 ; Min. 5544-52, 5583-9.
[3] W. Dig. p. 42 ; Min. 6913-44.
[4] W. Dig. p. 42 ; Min. 6945-55.

To these three reasons, we will presume to add a
fourth, *viz.*, that it is impossible to reduce the labour
ability, and capital invested, in any given undertaking,
to a common denominator for the purpose of comparing their respective values, unless it be assumed that
they are rewarded at the same rate. In comparing
wages with profits, therefore, we assume the very
point which the Socialists would institute the com-
parison in order to disprove. Hence it would seem
that mere statistics can never enable us to determine
the main matter in dispute between capital and
labour, *viz.*, how far is capital receiving too much and
labour too little ?

Instead of entering upon a profitless discussion of
the justice of the existing distribution of the rewards
of industry, it is now proposed to examine the evidence with a view to ascertaining the nature of the
practical issues involved, and the attitude of the rival
parties respecting them. In a word, it is proposed to
treat the problem of industrial remuneration from a
political and not from a mathematical point of view.

From a political point of view, the important
question is not whether the British workman's wages
are too high or too low, but whether he is asking for
more, and, if so, what is the precise nature of his
demand.

He is certainly asking for more, but the precise
nature of his demand requires some explanation. In
the first place, the evidence clearly shows—indeed, it
is a matter of common knowledge—that it is not a demand for Parliament to fix the rate of wages. Some
witnesses, it is true, would even go so far as that.

Thus, Mr. Keir Hardie, representing the Ayrshire Miners' Association, considered that employers should be forbidden to sell coal at a lower price than would enable them to pay a certain fixed minimum wage, and that the principle of fixing minimum rates and limiting production within the demand should be applied to all trades alike.[1] Mr. Friend, moreover, of the North of England Sailors' and Firemen's Union, desired foreigners to be prevented by law from working at lower wages than Englishmen,[2] and Mr. Ben Tillett thought that wages ought to be fixed for each trade at such a rate as would insure an ordinary standard of living to the workmen,[3] while Mr. T. Sutherst, who claimed to represent the omnibus drivers of London, contended that the principle of a "living wage" ought to be applied to all industries not affected by foreign competition.[4] Somewhat similar views were expressed by the representatives of the Amalgamated Society of Bakers, but, with these exceptions, scarcely a single responsible representative of a Trade Union claimed to have received a mandate to advocate the direct settlement of wages by Parliament, while most of them had received instructions to oppose it.

Several of the witnesses explained the opposition of the workmen as a class to a Wages Regulation Act, as follows:—Such an Act, they said in effect, must take one of two forms. It could either fix the *actual* rates, or it could fix the *minimum* rates payable to the vari-

[1] A. II. Dig. p. 28 ; Min. 12588-9.
[2] B. I. Dig. pp. 39-40 ; Min. 10400-6.
[3] B. I. Dig. p. 16 ; Min. 3922.
[4] B. II. Dig. p. 65 ; Min. 16102-21.

ous classes of workmen. If the actual rates were to be stated, they must be placed either at too low a figure to satisfy the workmen during good times, or at too high a figure to save many of the employers from bankruptcy during bad times, thereby increasing the number of unemployed members on the Trade Union funds. And if the *minimum* rates were to be stated, employers would refuse to pay higher rates than the minimum during good times in order to recoup themselves for being obliged to pay as high rates as the minimum during bad. Not that the workmen do not want greater stability in their earnings. On the contrary, they do desire it most earnestly. But they recognise that, so long as employment is dependent upon the employers earning a profit, so long is it expedient, not to fix wages, but to make them respond more readily to the fluctuations of the market. An Act of Parliament, they appear to think, might have the effect of throwing them out of work altogether in bad times, while preventing the rise of wages that would normally take place when trade is good.

The Socialists, of course, contend that under State control the fluctuations of trade would be prevented, and, in that case, the above arguments would not apply. Mr. Sidney Webb, indeed, with his characteristic habit of clothing Radical proposals in a Conservative dress—thus, he described an Eight Hours' Law as a mere amendment to the Factory Acts— stated that the value of the relief given under the Poor Law practically fixed a minimum legal wage at the present time, inasmuch as no man would long continue to work at a smaller wage than the State would give him without working at all. But even Mr. Webb did not include a Wages Regulation Act in his programme of immediate reform.[1]

Curiously enough, one of the most urgent pleas for fixing a legal minimum wage came from the lips of an employer. Mr. G. Green, a nail manufacturer and a member of the Dudley Chamber of Commerce, said :— "The periodical strikes that occur in connection with this industry, though generally for an advance of wages, do not imply unpleasant contentions between employers and employed. On the contrary, they are usually suspensions of work, mutually arranged between the two parties, with a view to raising the rates of wages and prices when brought to a dangerously low level by the competition both in the labour and in the nail markets. Working, as they usually do, on speculation, instead of merely to order, as was the practice twenty years ago, the workpeople cannot sell all their nails to the manufacturers from whom they have purchased the iron. They are, accordingly, obliged to pass them on to "foggers" or middlemen, who pay only such a price as will enable them to undersell, to the extent of from 5 to 15 per cent., those workers that offer nails to the manufacturers directly. By this means, the earnings of the nail-makers tend to fall lower and lower, and the manufacturers are obliged to take advantage of it by the severity of the competition among themselves. At last, wages reach the lowest point the workpeople can bear, and an advance becomes imperative. No manufacturer, however, dares to concede it without a guarantee that his

---

[1] W. Dig. p. 22 ; Min. 3779, 3782-3, 4468-71, 4480-2,

rivals will do the same. The employers, therefore, on being appealed to by the workers, urge them to organise a general strike for the advance throughout the trade. This has the desired effect of raising wages and prices temporarily; but the same evil conditions continue to exist, and soon begin once more to produce the same evil result. Now, though the employers act jointly in the matter of wages, in fact they will never concede advances individually, they have no specific organisation, and, though the men are attempting to form one with the help of the employers, they will probably never have sufficient confidence in themselves to carry it out. Failing organisation, therefore, to which both employers and employed would naturally look for a means of remedying the above-mentioned evils, Parliament should either itself fix, or empower county and municipal councils to fix, a minimum rate of wages."[1]

Mr. Green's views on this point, however, are quite exceptional. Otherwise, we should not have quoted them so fully. The large majority of the representatives of all classes in the industrial world concurred in expressing emphatic disapproval of State action in fixing the rates of wages.

Now, though the workers desire the Government to do nothing towards fixing the rates of wages as a Government, they want it to do a great deal as an employer of labour. All the Socialist and Trade Union representatives that referred to the subject agreed in thinking that it ought to lead rather than follow the market in determining the wages of its

[1] A. III. Dig. p. 17 ; Min. 19999-20002.

employés. It should always pay the full Trade Union
rates, and should take care that its contractors did the
same. This point was brought very prominently
forward by the Socialists, who could not but feel that
the grievances of Government employés constituted a
standing argument against their favourite thesis that
industrial functions are better discharged by political
than by purely industrial bodies.

Again, though the witnesses did not desire Government to fix the actual rates or even the minimum
rates that other employers were to pay, they did not
mean that it should not regulate the payment of wages
at all. On the contrary, they wished to increase the
stringency of the various Acts by which the manner,
time and place, though not the rates, of payment are
regulated already.

First, as to the manner. Payments in kind and
deductions from wages in respect of allowances are
already prohibited by the Truck Acts, 1831 and 1887,
in the case of most manual labourers. If, however,
the allowances consist of medicine and doctor's bills,
fodder for horses and cattle used in the course of
employment, tenancy of houses, or meals to be eaten
on the premises, then deductions may be made in
respect of them from the wages, provided that a clause
to that effect be inserted in the contract of hiring.
Deductions may also be made for sharpening and
repairing tools, but only by a written agreement not
forming part of the contract of hiring. The representatives of the West of Scotland miners desired
deductions for repairing tools, and doctors' fees, and
all deductions that a jury might consider unreasonable

to be prohibited.   Mr. Fretwell,[1] representing the
Spring Knife Cutlers' Union of Sheffield, thought
that no deductions ought to be allowed for workroom,
gas, power, and the use of tools.   On the other hand,
Mr. Glennie, representing the Amalgamated Society of
Engineers, considered that every workman should be,
not merely permitted, but compelled to submit to a
certain deduction from his wages, for the purpose of
purchasing shares in his employer's business at par,
when the aggregate amount deducted reached a certain
figure.[2]

Secondly, with reference to the time of payment, it
was proposed by Mr. Wilkie, representing the Associated Shipwrights' Society, that the official receiver
or trustee should be empowered to advance, on the
security of the assets in the estate of a bankrupt employer, the wages, which are already a preferential
claim, on the date at which they became due, instead
of waiting for the commencement of the wind-
ing up.[3]

Lastly, with reference to the place of payment, it
was desired by Mr. Falvy, representing the South Side
Labour Protection League, to make offences under the
Payment of Wages in Public-houses Prohibition Act,
1883, punishable by imprisonment instead of by fine ;[4]
and Mr. T. Homer, representing the Cradley Heath and
District Chainmakers' Society, wanted the giving of
orders as well as the payment of wages in public-

[1] A. II. Min. 19634-43, 19695-8, 19767-8.
[2] A. III. Min. 23116-31.
[3] A. III. Min. 21467-71.
[4] B. I. Min. 2793-4,

houses to be made illegal.[1] On the other hand, Mr. Falvy considered that a member of a gang of workmen should cease to be liable for paying his fellows in a public-house, such liability being allowed to rest solely upon the employer; and he contended that a publican should only be held liable for permitting the Act to be broken, if it was proved that he was aware that wages were being paid illegally under his roof.[2]

So much, then, for the action of the State in relation to wages. The remaining portion of this chapter we propose to devote to the evidence relating to sliding scales, or devices by which the variations in the rates of wages are automatically adjusted, and to profit sharing, or the system by which variations in wages—though not in earnings—might be rendered unnecessary.

The account given by the witnesses, representing the mining and iron industries, of the general nature and working of sliding scales, was to the following effect:—" A sliding scale," they explained, " is a method by which wages rise or fall an agreed percentage with every agreed rise or fall in the price, such price being ascertained at fixed intervals from the books of a given number of employers by accountants chosen respectively by employers and employed. The relation which the rate of wages had borne to the selling price over a previous period of some duration is ascertained, and the scale is based

[1] A. II. Dig. p. 54; 55; Min. 16967-70, 17000-3,
17184-93.
[2] B. I. Min. 2793-4.

upon this relation. The price agreed upon is the 'standard' price, and the corresponding wage is the 'standard' wage. The scale is guaranteed to operate for a certain period, and is then terminable, generally speaking, by a three months' notice from either side; but otherwise, if neither party is dissatisfied, the scale continues in operation, subject to the stipulated notice. The scales are, however, modified from time to time, because considerations other than the price of the product, such as the condition of the labour market and other matters affecting the cost of production, after a certain period, interfere with the basis."

From this it is clear that the working of a sliding scale presupposes organisation on both sides. The accountants, whose duty it is to ascertain the prices and so to settle when and to what extent an alteration in the rates of wages is to take place, must be paid by somebody. And the payment of the men's accountant presupposes the collection of a common fund. Again, when "considerations other than the price of the product" begin to affect the cost of production and so render the scale unfair, there must be a joint board of employers and employed to draw up a fresh scale, or else the aggrieved party will give notice to terminate it altogether. And the members of the board must have definite constituencies. It is, therefore, only in those industries where organisation is strong, and where "collective bargaining" is a fixed habit, that sliding scales can work, and, as a matter of fact, it is only in the mining and the iron trades that they have ever been really successful.

The advantages of a sliding scale are obvious. In

the first place, it settles the entire class of questions that are likely to prove most contentious once for all, or, at any rate, once for several months, and, by so doing, prevents many a quarrel, and lightens the labour and expense of the joint boards. In the second place, it prevents wages from fluctuating too violently. As was pointed out by Mr. Weeks, representing the Northumberland coal owners, the absence of a sliding scale enables the men to resist the slight reductions that become necessary from time to time, and thus compels the employers, when times are very bad indeed, to insist upon a large reduction all at once, " whereupon the men get their backs up and strike." [1] Thirdly, under a sliding scale, fluctuations in wages are always several weeks behind the fluctuations in prices, so that both parties have plenty of warning, and can set their house in order accordingly. This is an especial advantage to employers in preparing their tenders for contracts.

But, with all these advantages, sliding scales are very difficult to work. In the first place, it is very difficult to draw them up on a fair basis, and, in complex industries, where the commodities produced are various, and the relation of their prices to the value of the labour expended in producing them, is more various still, what was difficult before becomes impossible. Again, to preserve the relation between wages and prices is not always the same thing as preserving the relation between wages and profits. And it is difficult to draft a scale which will satisfy the men and at the same time make it the employer's interest

[1] A. I. Dig. p. 19 ; Min. 3075-7.

to see prices rise.   To be successful, therefore, a scale must not merely fix the proportion being wages and prices, but must provide for a shifting of that proportion in its extreme ranges.   That is to say, when prices are very high, the pace at which wages rise relatively to those prices must be accelerated.   And, conversely, when prices are exceptionally low, the pace at which wages fall relatively to those prices must be slackened.   Again, care must be taken to make provision for a sufficiently wide range of prices.   Very often sliding scales fail because prices rise or fall beyond their limits altogether.   It will be readily understood, therefore, that the drafting of a fair and workable scale demands the greatest possible experience of the vicissitudes of the trade on the part of those to whom it is entrusted.

And, when the scale has once been drafted, it is by no means easy to persuade the men to abide by it. This is especially the case when prices are rising, and the advances of wages under the scale are several weeks behind.

In some cases, moreover, it has a bad effect upon the membership of the Trade Unions.   The men organise in order to get their wages raised, and, when a sliding scale is established, they are apt to think that the Union has no longer any *raison d'être.*   Thus, the representatives of the Cleveland Miners' Association informed the Commission that, during the two years that a sliding scale was in operation, one half of the members resigned.[1]   Such cases, however, must be regarded as exceptional.   Most organisations that

[1] A. I. Dig. p. 12 ; Min. 1171, 1234, 1245.

are strong enough to create sliding scales are strong enough to survive them.

Furthermore, a sliding scale can never be permanent. The proportion between wages and prices must be re-adjusted according as the market value of labour varies relatively to the market value of commodities. But, though a single scale cannot last for ever, Mr. Whitwell considered that the system whereby scales were worked and renewed by the North of England Conciliation Board had a very fair prospect of permanency.[1]

Profit-sharing may be defined as a system of industrial remuneration whereby wages are supplemented by the payment of bonuses bearing a certain ratio to the profits as determined by agreement between the employer and his workpeople. In other words, it is a device for minimising the fluctuations in the profits and wages themselves by throwing them upon a third fund, created *ad hoc*, in which both parties have an equal interest. Thus, wages are paid at a fixed rate, and profits are paid at a fixed rate, and what is left is divided between the wage and profit earners respectively.

It is obvious, therefore, that, in order to work at all, neither profits nor wages must be fixed at so high a figure as to leave nothing in the third fund to be divided. It is often said that profit-sharing schemes have failed, because the workmen will not share losses as well as profits. The real fact is that the authors of such schemes have never provided any machinery by which losses could be shared. If the balance in

[1] A. II. Dig. p. 103 ; Min. 15016, 18025.

hand is just sufficient to pay the fixed sum to profits
and wages and no more, the profit-sharing machinery
has no work to do; while, if the balance is not
sufficient to pay both profits and wages, there is work
to do which the profit-sharing machinery cannot perform. The workmen have already received their
wages and spent them; the employer, who has been
waiting for his profits, must, therefore, suffer the whole
loss. When this happens, it is surely a misrepre-
sentation to say that the workmen, on having losses to
face, abandon the profit-sharing scheme. Say rather
that the profit-sharing scheme is defective.

This alone would be sufficient objection to the proposal made by Mr. Maxwell, representing the Scottish
Co-operative Wholesale Society, that it would be desirable to entirely supersede the wages system by the
system of profit-sharing.[1] Every such system yet
propounded demands an established and successful
business; and, as it is hardly necessary to point out,
this condition is by no means always fulfilled, and can
be fulfilled only by a complete cessation of enterprise.
Again, every such scheme depends upon the payment
of the workers' subsistence out of some other fund.
Wages could never be abolished except in the case of
workers who were also capitalists. But, granted that
wages could be entirely superseded, the workmen
would never consent to trust entirely to their bonuses,
unless they had a strong organisation to bargain with
their employer as to the basis of the apportionment
and to check his profit and loss account. And a
strong Trade Union is apt to view with jealousy any

[1] W. Dig. p. 12; Min. 631-2.

system which, by concentrating the workmen's interest in preserving the profit fund intact, tends to weaken its hold over its own members. As was pointed out in a preceding chapter, the Trade Unions wish to draw labour and capital together, but only if they are themselves essential to the alliance. For all these reasons, it is, as Mr. Giffen pointed out, unlikely that profit-sharing will solve the whole problem of industrial remuneration.[1]

Inasmuch, however, as profit-sharing seeks only to supplement, and not to supersede, the wages system, strong organisation is not essential to its working. Of the present total of 77 profit-sharing firms, the largest is the South Metropolitan Gas Company, which employs only non-unionist workers. In this case, indeed, the workers have accepted it, not only without having a Trade Union at their back, but though it was designedly started to prevent them organising. Just before the great strike of 1889, the Company invited its employés to sign an agreement by which each man should receive 1 per cent. on his year's wages for every 1d. reduction below 2s. 8d. per 1000 feet of gas, on consideration that no money should be withdrawn within the first five years, and that the share of any man leaving the service without permission should be forfeited. Upon the objection of the Union, these last clauses, which would practically have relieved the employer of all fear of strikes, and so deprived the men of their only weapon, were withdrawn, but not until 1000 non-Union men had signed the agreement including them, and it appears

[1] W. Dig. p. 43; Min. 6995-6.

from documentary evidence handed in by Mr. Livesey, that the agreement still provides that " the workman shall stay a certain number of months in the service . . . . . except by special permission from the engineer of the station at which he may, for the time being, be employed." [1] The scheme is, therefore, still a means of insurance against Trade Unionism and strikes, and its mode of working can be practically dictated by the Company. The workmen, however, support it, because, apart from the scheme, the Company pays the full Trade Union rates of wages, and there would consequently be nothing to gain by refusing to accept the bonuses.

Profit-sharing, moreover, is not consistently opposed by the Trade Unions. Thus, Mr. Whitburn, representing the Enginemen's and Firemen's Union, expressed himself in its favour,[2] as also did the representatives of the Amalgamated Society of Bakers, and Mr. J. H. Jolley, representing the Cork United Trades' Society,[3] while Mr. R. Manton, representing the National Federation of Fishermen, said that the 2000 of his constituents that were paid out of the profits considered they would lose caste by working under any other system.[4] On the other hand, the representatives of the Scotch Typographical Association and several other Unions, considered that the bonuses did not compensate the men for the extra exertion they encouraged them to put forth, besides causing a

[1] C. III. App. 52.
[2] A. II. Dig. pp. 41, 42 ; Min. 17331, 17417-25, 17478-82.
[3] C. II. Dig. p. 53 ; Min. 17131-5.
[4] B. I. Dig. p. 43 ; Min. 11239.

smaller number to be employed. Mr. Fenwick, representing the Parliamentary Committee of the Trade Union Congress, pointed out that, in fluctuating trades, the men were generally hostile to profit-sharing, because they thought that, by allowing a higher rate of interest to capital in order to cover the loss during times of depression, which they themselves cannot share, they were causing a proportionate reduction in wages. " They may also," he added, " be influenced by the fact that they would be able, during good times, to make a better bargain in securing advances in wages than they are able to make under a profit-sharing scheme." [1] Be this as it may, it is clear that the natural attitude of Trade Unions towards profit-sharing is one of hostility. Being essentially organisations for appreciating wages at the expense of profits, they could hardly be expected to welcome with cordiality a scheme which gives the workman an interest in the integrity of the profit fund. That they do so sometimes, can only be out of deference to the individual feelings of their members, who are not slow to appreciate the many unquestionable advantages which profit-sharing, under favourable circumstances, affords. In fact, the attitude of the Unions towards profit-sharing is to be explained on the same ground as their attitude towards the co-operative societies.

How closely the principles of co-operation and profit-sharing are connected has already been noted. In fact, a certain kinship of principle may be traced between all the following methods of remuneration—

[1] W. Dig. 27 ; Min. 7475-6.

E

co-operative production, where the workers monopolise both profits and management ; industrial
partnership, where they share, but do not monopolise
them ; profit-sharing, where they share in profits, but
not in management ; gain-sharing, or associated piecework, where groups of men share in such portion of
the profits only as is derived from economy in labour ;
and piecework proper, where individuals are paid
according to the value of their work. All these are
methods of payment by result, and therefore out of a
different fund from the wages which are advanced
before the result is achieved. For this reason, it is
the natural instinct of the Trade Unions to oppose
them ; and the evidence given by their representatives
before the Commission proves that, in the absence of
any special reason to the contrary, they generally do.

CHAPTER II.

HOURS OF LABOUR.[1]

Whence the Demand for regulating the Hours of Adult
Male Labour proceeds—The Motives of the Demand—How
far is it a Demand for Higher Prices?—How far is it a
Demand for the Absorption of the Unemployed?—Should
the Hours be regulated by organised Effort or by Act of
Parliament?—How should an Act regulating the Hours of
Labour be drafted?

So much has been said and written in recent years on
the subject of the "eight hours day," that it might
well be doubted whether the Commission could have
anything fresh to say on the well-worn theme. The
portion of the Report dealing with the hours of labour,
however, will probably be read with interest, and the
evidence on which it is based certainly enables us to
apprehend more clearly the true nature of an issue
which has been well-nigh overwhelmed by much
talk. The issue is a complex one, but it becomes confused
only when treated as if it were too simple. If care be
taken to deal separately and in order with each one
of the questions involved, all difficulty will disappear.

[1] This chapter is chiefly based upon the abstracts of evidence
on the eight hours' day, which are incorporated in the digests.

First, then, let us inquire whence the demand for a regulation of the hours of labour proceeds. It does not represent the unanimous voice of the workers. It does not proceed from any of the 6,000,000 non-unionist workers, who, whether from principle or from force of circumstances, do not demand any system of industrial regulation whatever. It does not proceed from all even of the 1,000,000 Trade Unionists. Thus the representatives of the hand nail-makers', nut and bolt makers', and coopers' organisations, and of the Boot and Shoe Operatives' Union, informed the Commission that neither employers nor employed could exist under any system of regulations that prevented them from making up in good times for their losses incurred in periods of depression. In some cases, moreover, where the Union officials are in favour of regulating and reducing the hours, the members themselves are opposed to it. Thus, Mr. Trow, representing the Associated Iron and Steel Workers' Union of Great Britain, said that an attempt on the part of an employer, acting in conjunction with the Union executive, to introduce an eight hours' day in his works, had recently failed owing to the determined opposition of the men, who positively refused to work under the new arrangement.[1] In most Unions, finally, where there is a majority of members in favour of regulation, there is a strong minority against it. In spite of this, however, it seems that the principle of depriving the individual of his full freedom of contract in settling his hours of labour is accepted by the

[1] A. II. Dig. p. 91 ; Min. 15232-41, 15311-9, 15349-50, 15403-6, 15450-6.

bulk of the Trade Unionists in the country. Indeed, as Mr. Mann pointed out, such freedom is irrevocably lost already, inasmuch as modern business establishments can be conducted only on the basis of uniformity in the men's hours of labour.[1] The individual has practically no voice in determining how long he is to work; he must work either the same hours as his fellows or not at all.

Evidence in favour of the principle of regulation was, accordingly, given by the representatives of the following classes of workmen : miners, blast-furnacemen, enginemen and firemen, locksmiths, whitesmiths and cutlers, dockers, seamen, omnibus and tram drivers, railway servants, workers in textile trades, hosiers, boat clickers, carpenters, masons, painters, cabinetmakers, chemical-workers, coach-makers, gas-workers, printers and bakers. Their advocacy, however, varied greatly in warmth, and was prompted by widely different motives.

With some Unions, the demand for shorter hours was really equivalent to a demand for raising the cost of production ; but, with the large majority, it was motived by a desire to multiply vacancies, and so to get their unemployed members off their funds. The two objects should be kept quite distinct. Those that had the former in view preferred their demand most strongly during good times, while those that had the latter in view preferred their demand most strongly during periods of depression. In the one case, it was a demand for leisure ; in the other, it was a demand for work. In the one case, moreover, it

[1] W. Dig. p. 17.

was a demand for establishments to be closed ; in the other, it was a demand for establishments to remain open. In the one case, in fact, it was desired to prevent the absorption of the unemployed, which, in the other, it was desired to secure.

Bearing this in mind, the reader will be prepared for the following curious fact. When it came to be argued whether the regulation of hours would have the effect of increasing the cost of production, and whether it would have the effect of absorbing the unemployed, those that desired to raise the cost of production said it would not absorb the unemployed ; and those that desired to absorb the unemployed contended that it would not increase the cost of production.

Obviously, the former had in their mind the ceasing of all work at a certain hour, less production, and higher prices ; while the latter contemplated the introduction of a second shift, greater production and lower prices. The former hoped that- the higher prices would not prove so prohibitive as to check demand ; the latter hoped that the lower prices would be compensated for by a wider demand sufficiently to prevent wages being reduced. The former, however, were prepared, if demand were checked, to let the least fortunate lose employment in order that the rest should be more highly paid ; and the latter were prepared, if wages were reduced, to accept the reduction in order that the unemployed should be absorbed.

Such, then, being the nature of the two radically different demands for regulation of hours, let us see by whom they were respectively made, and by what arguments they were supported and criticised. The only important class of workmen that desire shorter hours in order to raise wages by increasing the cost of production, are the miners. Their point of view was most clearly expressed by Mr. A. Onions of the South Wales and Monmouthshire Miners' Association, who said :—" Life is before cost, and the price of the commodity must be raised in order to increase the safety of the mine, and be conducive to the safety of the miners as a whole,"[1] and especially by Mr. Small, representing the Lanarkshire miners, whose evidence may be reproduced as follows :—" Rise in price might damage the export trade, but the sooner we get rid of that the better. Too much mining is done. The employers' objection to assisting the men to regulate the output proceeds from want of enlightenment. They conceive that the more trade they do, the more they will make, whereas the opposite is the case. A smaller output would give a better price, better wages and higher profits. And it is now common knowledge that we are depleting the country of minerals, and by and by we shall run short, while the continental nations are saving their mineral wealth. The export trade of coal is about 22 out of 170 millions, and this is sufficient to considerably affect prices. But matters could be adjusted by the workmen limiting the supply, and producing for home consumption instead of for foreign competition. The miners are now beginning to see that their strongest weapon is to withhold the supplies, and, in future, the price of coal will be determined, not so much by the

[1] A. II. Dig. p. 51 ; Min. 5247-52.

necessities of the trade, as by the action of the miners
in limiting the output, and many of the employers
are coming round to the same view."[1]

The miners may be said to stand almost alone in
taking this view of the matter. It is not surprising,
therefore, to hear from Mr. Fenwick, who represented
the Parliamentary Committee of the Trade Union
Congress, that they objected to their case being dealt
with in the same Hours of Labour Bill as other industries, and insisted on promoting a separate Bill
of their own.[2] And not only do the miners stand
alone in this matter, but they are not by any means
unanimous among themselves. The miners in Durham
and Northumberland, indeed, strongly object to their
hours being interfered with. As their representatives
explained, the " hewers " or actual coal getters, who
are in a majority of the persons employed, work less
than the proposed eight hours limit already, and, inasmuch as the amount of work they can do is determined by the amount of work done by the already
insufficient number of subsidiary workers, who now
work about ten hours a day, they are afraid that, if
the hours of the latter were reduced to eight, they
would either have to do a portion of the unskilled
work themselves at a lower rate of payment than they
get for " hewing," or else that their own hours would
have to be reduced to six per day. And, being paid
by the piece, they would thereby lose more than they
could ever hope to gain by the higher wages to be

[1] A. II. Dig. p. 87 ; Min. 10233, 10308-42, 10495.
[2] W. Dig. p. 26, 27 ; Min. 7204-20.

derived from higher prices, the result of diminished production.

These arguments were said not to apply to the hewers in other districts, for two reasons. First, that they work more than eight hours already; and secondly, that they already have to do a large portion of the unskilled work, which their fellows in Northumberland and Durham wish to avoid. And, rightly or wrongly, they think that a reduction of their hours to eight per day *would* be compensated for by the higher wages to be derived from higher prices, the result of diminished production.

Even in Durham and Northumberland, moreover, there is a large minority, consisting chiefly of the subsidiary workers, who desire the hours to be reduced. They were represented by Mr. G. Jacques, who asserted that, were it not for the opposition of the Union officials, there would be found, even in the northern coalfield, a majority of the miners in favour of the Mines Eight Hours Bill promoted by the Unions in other districts.[1] In the Cleveland district, *i.e.*, South Durham and North Yorkshire, moreover, the Miners' Unions were in favour of a reduction in the hours of boys and subsidiary workers, though not in those of "hewers."

The main body of the miners certainly act up to their professions. It appeared from the evidence relating to the South Wales coalfield, that they frequently absented themselves from work in order to prevent coal becoming too plentiful, and Mr. Keir Hardie, representing the miners in the West of Scot-

[1] A. I. Dig. p. 21 ; Min. 3697-701.

land district, said :—" In 1886, the stronger men voluntarily limited their labour to the production of 2s. 6d. worth of coal a day, in order to carry out the principle of an eight hours' day, and to raise the rate of wages. No longer being able to expand the productive power of their hands so as to supply exceptional demands, the employers were prevented from accepting specially large orders and lowering their prices in order to obtain them. Prices, indeed, were not only maintained, but raised, and a corresponding increase in the rate of wages was the result."[1] This evidence was afterwards confirmed by Mr. Baird, who represented the coalowners in the same district.[2]

With the exception of the miners, the members of no important industry seem to desire a reduction of hours for the sole purpose of taxing the public. Even the railway men, who have not only promoted, but actually succeeded in passing an Act dealing with their hours, do not expect whatever additional cost it may entail to be thrown upon the travelling public. Their idea seems to be that it must rest with the shareholders, because fares are fixed, irrespectively of the working expenses, at the figure that will yield the largest gross receipts. Whatever be the economic effect of a reduction of hours, moreover, the railway workers desire it, like members of other trades, partly for the purpose of absorbing their unemployed, and partly because their long hours are in themselves a great grievance. The subject, however, is fully dealt with in the chapter relating to transport trades.

[1] A. II. Dig. p. 26 ; Min. 13220-4, 13366-74.
[2] A. II. Dig. p. 30 ; Min. 13462-5.

In the iron, engineering, and cognate trades, shorter hours are being demanded by the following organisations: the blast furnacemen's, the enginemen's and firemen's, and the locksmiths' Unions, the Sheffield Federated Trades' Council, and the Unions connected with shipbuilding trades. In the case of the blast furnacemen, the Union receives only a half-hearted support from those of its members that work by the piece. At the same time, their hours are very long— in some cases 90 a week—and, especially in regard to Sunday work, are felt to be a great grievance by the majority of the men. The other Unions in this group desired the hours to be regulated in order to absorb their unemployed members who are prevented from working by the selfishness of their fellows in doing overtime. Many had enacted rules restricting overtime, but found it more or less difficult to enforce them.

The desire to absorb the unemployed was also put prominently forward by the representatives of the Unions connected with the various transport trades, the dockers', seamen's, and firemen's, omnibus and tramworkers', etc. And it was this group of trades that gave the Eight Hours' Movement the most unqualified measure of support.

The representatives of the textile, clothing, building, chemical, printing, and other miscellaneous trades, also, were anxious to get their unemployed members absorbed by a reduction of hours; but all in this last group betrayed a greater or less tendency to be frightened of the result. They had foreign competition to face, even carpentry work being imported from abroad, and they were very much afraid of

having either to accept less than a " living wage," or
to see their work taken from them. Nearly every
Union, in short, appeared to be in this dilemma.
Having enrolled a larger number of members than the
trade could accommodate in order to prevent wages
being lowered by the competition of non-Unionist
labour, they were compelled either to expend all
their funds in support of their unemployed members,
or to adopt a policy which would seriously diminish
the power of their employed members to pay their
subscriptions.

It is not surprising, therefore, to find that many of
the Unions in this group viewed the Eight Hours'
Movement—with favour, indeed,—but absolutely
without enthusiasm. Thus, Mr. Ham, representing the
Alliance Cabinet Makers' Association, said: "We shall
have to come eventually, I suppose, to the regulation
of the hours of labour by Act of Parliament."[1] The
Lancashire textile workers seemed to find special
difficulty in choosing between the two evils. On the
whole, however, they decided in favour of a reduction of hours, hoping that a similar reduction would
soon be made in the hours worked by their rivals
abroad.

As has already been pointed out, the support of the
workmen to the Eight Hours' Movement is largely
based on the hope that the greater efficiency of the
workers would enable them to earn as much with the
shorter hours as they do now. Possibly each man
might be able to produce the same output. But, if
he did, *the unemployed would not be absorbed at all,*

[1] C. II. Dig. p. 80; Min. 19850-2.

for the demand for goods would not be increased by increasing the productiveness of the workers. The unemployed exist in this country because the power of English labour to produce is in excess of the power of foreign nations to purchase. Shorter hours might increase our production of marketable articles, but it would not increase the number of our markets.

This argument was put very prominently forward by Mr. Gerald Balfour in cross-examining Mr. Tom Mann. It can be parried only by acknowledging its force. It was, accordingly, contended in reply that, although it might be true that the increased efficiency that was hoped for would prevent the absorption of the permanently unemployed, whose lack of work was due to chronic over-production, the regulation of hours, by making the productive machinery less elastic, would help to check the fluctuations of trade that threw other men out of employment intermittently, and, as these were the men that came upon the Union funds, the Unions would be quite content if these alone were kept at work. Again, the hope that the average production per man would be maintained with shorter hours, was only too likely to be disappointed, in which case—so it was contended—a reduction of wages, if not too severe, would be borne for the sake of the absorption, which, in that case, would certainly result.

Besides, there was a further hope that the reduction in wages, which was agreed to be the *natural* effect of a diminished production per worker, might be prevented. " Organised effort," it was urged, might be sufficient to maintain wages at their present figure at

the expense of profits and interest. In some cases, no
doubt, the employers and capitalists would contrive
to throw the burden upon the public in the form of
higher prices; but they would not be able to do so
always, because demand is relative to a certain price,
and it would not pay them to check demand. If they
did raise prices and so checked demand, it was admitted that the desired absorption of the unemployed
would once more be frustrated, but it was argued by
Mr. Tom Mann that the tendency of prices to rise
might be forcibly counteracted by State management
of industry, and that, if the worst came to the worst,
the reduction of wages might be accepted. But low
wages would not be the general advantage of the community. If the capitalists would consent to maintain
the rates of payment, they would be amply repaid by
the increased purchasing power of the workers, which
would constitute an increased demand. It is true—
Mr. Mann continued—that the increased expenditure
of the wage earners would be partly compensated for
by decreased expenditure on the part of the capitalists;
but the latter would not cut down their personal expenses to the same extent as the wage earners would
raise theirs; so that an increased national consumption would be the net result to the ultimate advantage of all concerned.[1]

Assuming the demand for a regulation of hours to
be valid and justified—a point on which there is still
considerable room for doubt—two questions remain
to be considered. First, whether that regulation
should necessarily be *State* regulation, applied by Act

[1] W. Dig. p. 17.

of Parliament, and, next, how should the Act be
drafted ? The only alternative to State regulation is
Trade Union regulation, and this is already applied
in many cases, *e.g.*, in the engineering and shipbuilding trades. Mr. Webb contended that it was inexpedient to leave the matter to the Unions on three
important grounds—first, because their action is more
effective among well-organised workers than among
the less fortunate ones who need help the most.
Secondly, because it generally involves an expensive
strike, which, even if successful, leaves no guarantee
that the advantages gained in good times will not be
taken away in succeeding periods of depression. And,
thirdly, because it excludes an important party to the
transaction, *viz.*, the public, from a voice in the matter.
It is quite possible, he argued, for the Trade Unions
and the employers to mutually agree upon a shortening of hours, for the express purpose of taxing the
public, and an Act of Parliament is the only medium
through which the consent of the public to be so taxed
can be expressed.[1]

The view of the Trade Unions on the question is
that they do not like State interference where they
are able to help themselves; but, where they are
obviously too weak to obtain shorter hours, or, having
secured, to preserve them, there they are willing and,
in some cases, even anxious for the State to assist
them. The strongest and most wealthy of them, indeed—like the Associated Iron and Steel Workers'
and the Amalgamated Society of Engineers—will have
no State interference, even when they cannot get

[1] W. Dig. p. 22, ; Min. 4346-77.

their own way without it, but this is not the case with the majority.

The evidence given on this point by the representatives of the various Unions—excluding those that are not in favour of a reduction of hours at all—may be summarised as follows. The Cleveland Mining ssociation, which wants the hours of the boys and other subsidiary workers to be shortened, objects to State interference on the ground that, "if the men were to get what they wanted through Parliament, they would not take the trouble to join a Union."[1] The South Wales Miners' Associations are in favour of the hours being fixed by Parliament, because "a law is better than a strike."[2] The Scotch Miners' Associations desired legislation because they are too weak to enforce their own rules on the point. The Blast Furnacemen's Association holds that it would be better to get the hours reduced by Trade Union than by Parliamentary action, and by Parliamentary action than not at all. The Enginemen's and Firemen's Union prefers State interference, because "it would be impossible to reduce the hours permanently except by Act of Parliament, since, in bad times, employers must either reduce wages or lengthen hours in order to make a profit, and the men always prefer the latter alternative if left to their own devices, thereby increasing the number of unemployed members on the funds of the Union."[3] The Iron and Steel Workers'

[1] A. I. Dig. p. 12 ; Min. 1171, 1231, 1245.
[2] A. I. Dig. p. 52 ; Min. 4123-9.
[3] A. II. Dig. p. 42 ; Min. 17324-5, 17380-416, 17537-41, 17573-8.

Union holds that " the hours might be fixed by law if all men were of the same stature, strength and wits ; but, as they are not all cast in the same mould, Parliament is not justified in interfering. The Union officials know more about the wants of their own men in their own districts than all the members of Parliament."[1] The Locksmiths' Union desires Parliamentary action because it is not strong enough to deal effectively with the matter itself, especially in domestic workshops. The Sheffield Federated Trades' Council would support an Hours of Labour Bill, " to prevent the individual competing with the mass."[2] The Boilermakers', Engineers' and other Unions connected with the shipbuilding industry, where Trade Unionism is comparatively strong, and Socialism is, therefore, comparatively weak, consider that, inasmuch as the length of hours must be relative to the circumstances of the industry, an Hours of Labour Act would cause inconvenience and damage trade. The hours must, therefore, be shortened tentatively and by Trade Union action. The Union policy, accordingly, is to discourage overtime work in order to absorb the unemployed, and to discourage piecework in order to deprive the men of their interest in supporting overtime. Those members of the trades in question, however, that are employed in the Government arsenals and dockyards, having no fear of destroying the trade of *their* employer, are more inclined to look favourably upon legislative interference, and their Union—the Ship Constructive Association—has passed

[1] A. II. Dig. p. 47 ; Min. 15242-3.
[2] A. II. Dig. p. 92.

F

a resolution in support of a Bill to regulate the hours of labour.

The Unions connected with the transport trades are all in favour of State action, with the exception of the North of England Sailors' and Sea-going Firemen's Association, which has already succeeded by its own efforts in regulating the hours of its firemen, and hopes to be able to do the same for its sailors. It is, at least, highly doubtful whether any such regulation, whether by agreement or by law, could be applied to sailors in the merchant service, but the secretary of the Union above mentioned,[1] and the secretary of the National Amalgamated Sailors' and Firemen's Union, both maintained that it could. The Unions in this group of trades preferred State action, because to enforce rules of their own on the subject of hours seemed, at any rate for the moment, to be impossible.

Passing to the textile, clothing, and miscellaneous trades, we find most of the Unions so much occupied in considering whether shorter hours would or would not damage their industry, that the further question of whether the regulation should take the form of an Hours of Labour Act was almost disregarded. It was generally assumed, however, that an Act of Parliament would be necessary. There were, moreover, numerous exceptions to the general attitude of indecision. The Gas Workers' and General Labourers' Union, for example, was strongly in favour of a law being passed on the subject; but several of its branches, e.g. the lath-renders' section, where the men are

[1] B. I. Dig. p. 57; Min. 9914-5, 10425-39.

paid by the piece, " don't see nicely how it could be done." [1]

As to the form which an Hours of Labour Act should take, various proposals were made. Some were in favour of a general Act applying to all trades alike, others of an Act allowing trade option, and others of an Act allowing trade and district option combined. The representatives of most of the trades that desired legislation, however, did not seem to care what form it took, with two important provisos : first, that their own industry should be included ; secondly, that one portion of a trade should not be enabled to compete at an unfair advantage with the labour of other portions to which the Act applied. Trade option was, accordingly, accepted only in deference to the wishes of those trades that did not want an Act at all, while district option was accepted only in the case of trades .that served purely local markets. It was pointed out, however, that it was very difficult to formulate a definition of every trade, and still more difficult to determine what trades were purely local in their character.

The present instructions to the Parliamentary Committee of the Trade Union Congress contain no suggestion as to how these difficulties are to be over-come. They are merely : " To promote a Bill regulat-ing the hours of labour to eight per day, or 48 per week, in all trades and occupations, except mining,[2] which

[1] C. III. Dig. p. 136 ; Min. 23437.

[2] The exception as to mining was introduced in fulfilment of .the wish of the miners themselves, who did not want the pro-visions of the separate Bill that they were promoting on their own account to be tacked on to a Bill relating to other in-dustries.

Bill shall contain a clause enabling the organised members of any trade or occupation protesting by ballot against the same to be exempted from its provisions."

By combining the various suggestions made by Messrs. Tom Mann [1] and Sidney Webb,[2] however, it is possible to arrive at the following general plan :— That an Act should be passed empowering the Secretary of State responsible for the administration of the Factory Acts to make an order regulating the hours of any trade, and the local authorities to make an order regulating the hours of any portion of a trade within their jurisdiction, on petition from a majority of the workers concerned. Each trade or district should formulate its own definition. Thus, if a body of workers, desiring their hours to be reduced, felt that they could not safely petition for such a reduction unless it was to apply to their fellows in another trade or district also, they would be able to wait until concerted action could be arranged. Labourers employed in more industries than one would have a vote in connection with each; but this and all similar matters should be left to the trades themselves to settle. The Legislature should merely empower the Secretary of State and the municipalities to make— and perhaps to refuse to make—the orders or byelaws indicated. These orders, however, should in all cases strictly forbid the specified hours—which might be eight, or six, or ten, or any number—to be exceeded, except in cases of emergency, when employers should be able to apply for special leave.

[1] W. Dig. p. 17.

[2] W. Dig. p. 22 ; Min. 3747-8, 4413-7, 4437-40, 4453-67, 4507-27.

CHAPTER III.

EMPLOYERS' LIABILITY.

The Doctrine of Common Employment—Extent of Employers'
Liability—Proposed Extensions—Should Employers be
made General Insurers against Accidents?—Insurance Com-
panies—Contracting ˈOut—Effect of—Attitude of Trade
Unions towards—Immunity, not Compensation, demanded
—The Liability of the Employer *v.* the Liability of the
Negligent—Legal Procedure.

THE Government has, to some extent, anticipated the
Report of the Labour Commission by introducing the
Employers' Liability Bill, 1893, which embodied some
of the more important proposals made by the witnesses.
The Bill, however, comprehended neither the whole
of the law, nor the whole of the workmen's policy,
touching the liability of employers.

According to the common law, the liability of
masters with respect to the personal safety of their
servants was considered to arise solely from the terms
of the contract of service. And, in the absence of
express provision to the contrary, every such contract
was held to imply an undertaking on the part of the
master to exercise due care to associate his servants
with competent persons as mates and superiors. But
here the master's responsibility was held to cease.
Provided that he had exercised due care in the selection

85

of the members of his staff, he was not held liable for the results of their subsequent actions towards one another. The absence of such liability was expressed in positive language by the phrase, " The Doctrine of Common Employment," and it was to modify that doctrine that the existing Act of 1880 was passed, rendering the employer responsible in certain cases for the injuries caused by the negligence of foremen to inferior servants.

The labour representatives examined before the Commission were almost unanimously of opinion that the provisions of that Act were insufficient, and that the doctrine of common employment should be eliminated entirely.

This Mr. Asquith's Bill proposed to do. The first section provided that, " where, after the commencement of this Act, personal injury is caused to a workman by reason of the negligence of *any person* in the service of the workman's employer, the workman, or, in case of death, his representatives, shall have the same right to compensation and remedies against the employer as if the workman had not been a workman of, nor in the service of the employer, nor engaged in his work." That is to say, workmen were, in all cases, to be given the same right of action against their employers as the rule "*respondeat superior*" gives to members of the general public.

The Bill, moreover, proposed to extend the definition of the term " employer " so as to include the legal personal representatives of a deceased employer, and opened its benefits to merchant seamen, to Government employés other than soldiers and sailors, and to domestic and menial servants, to all of whom the Act of 1880 does not apply.

It also proposed to make the principal employer liable for the negligence of a sub-contractor or of a sub-contractor's servants. But it did not propose to make him liable in cases of pure accident, that is to say, in cases where negligence or failure on the part of some determinate person in the duty of taking reasonable care was not proved, and except that it provided in section 1, sub-section 2, that " a workman shall not be deemed to have accepted any risk incidental to his employment by reason only of his having entered upon, or continued in, the employment, after he knew of the risk," it did not propose to make him liable either in cases of acquiescence—that is to say, where the injured workman voluntarily encountered the risk—or in cases of contributory negligence—that is to say, where the injured workman was partially responsible for the existence of the danger.

One or other of the witnesses had proposed to extend the liability of employers to each of these cases. Thus, Mrs. Amie Hicks, representing the East London Ropemakers' Union, would make them liable in cases of pure accident;[1] Messrs. Quelch and Falvy,[2] representing the South Side Labour Protection League, wanted to make the pleas of acquiescence and contributory negligence valueless for the purpose of defence; while Mr. Davies, of the Amalgamated Society of Carpenters, desired the payment through employers of compensation for injuries of every kind

[1] C. I. Dig. p. 61 ; Min. 8348.
[2] B. I. Dig. p. 13.

to be enforced "as a general charge upon in- dustry."[1]

The extension of employers' liability to cases of pure accident was supported on the ground that, inasmuch as somebody must suffer, and the work that occasioned the accident was for the benefit of the employer, it would be more just for the employer to suffer than the worker. The pleas of acquiescence and contributory negligence, it was contended, should be made invalid, because they are of a quibbling nature and provable on such flimsy grounds as to be the source of great injustice. Petty negligence should not be allowed to excuse the grave negligence to which it may contribute.

Mr. Davies' suggestion to make compensation for accidents a general charge upon industry is resolvable into two propositions, one containing a proposal, and the other an argument. The proposal is to make employers liable to pay compensation for all injuries indiscriminately, and the argument is that this will not be hard on them, because they will be able to recoup themselves by charging higher prices to their customers; or, in other words, because employers' liability is a tax, not upon profits, but upon production.

Of course, this argument may be said to prove nothing. For the justice of a measure is not proved by showing that it will do no harm to A because he will be able to shift the burden on to B. On the other hand, it may be said to prove too much. For it suggests, first, that the very principle of employers' liability may not be quite fully justified in any case,

[1] C. II. Dig. p. 96 ; Min. 18247.

if, in extreme cases, it has to be explained away, and, secondly, that an employers' liability, which is justifiable only on the ground that it is really public insurance and not employers' liability at all, may be a little hard on the public. In short, it may be said to raise the question whether, in this matter of employers' liability, the workman's legal rights are not already in advance of his moral rights against both his employers and the community.

Now, it would be possible to make out a very good case against the justice of holding employers, as such, liable at all. For it should never be forgotten that, besides the liability of the employer, there exists the liability of the actual tortfeasor, *i.e.*, the person whose negligence caused the accident, be he employer, foreman, contractor or fellow-servant. According to the common law, the employer was liable, not because he was an employer, but because he was a person guilty of negligence ; and, as was pointed out by Mr. J. Price, the general manager of the firm of Messrs. Palmer & Co., Limited, shipbuilders, it would be absurd to call an employer negligent because the members of his staff did not possess in absolute perfection the qualities of competency and carefulness in virtue of which he had engaged them.[1] The common law recognises this by attributing the negligence of a negligent employer to himself, and the negligence of a negligent workman to himself. Where, then, it may be asked, is the justice of supplementing the equitable, ancient, and unrepealed doctrine of the liability of the negligent by the indefensible, novel and redundant doctrine of the liability of the employer?

[1] A. III. Dig. p. 86 ; Min. 26448-62.

On abstract grounds, this argument has never been completely refuted, and it will, therefore, always furnish employers with a pretext, if not with a good reason, not only for resisting extensions of their liability, but also for seeking to reduce it. Thus, Mr. W. Beckett Hill, representing the firm of Messrs. Allan Bros. & Co., shipowners, contended that employers should be held liable only for such injuries as result directly from orders given by themselves or their representatives, and from defective gear.[1] On practical grounds, however, much remains to be said on the other side. It may be urged, first, that the liability of negligent persons other than the employer, is of no practical value, because they are seldom rich enough to pay compensation. This fact is recognised by the common law in cases where the plaintiff is a member of the general public, and it is unjust to withhold from workmen as a class a benefit conceded to the community as a whole. Again, it may be urged that the justice of the applications of the principles of employers' liability which have already been sanctioned is so firmly established that arguments based on the injustice of the principle itself are irrelevant. And, above all, it may be argued that the principle in question is conceded already. As Mr. Price, of the firm of Messrs. Palmer & Co., shipbuilders, stated, the doctrine of common employment is the only contradiction to the theory that employers' liability is equivalent to insurance,[2] and, by the passing of the Act of 1880, the doctrine of common employ-

[1] B. I. Dig. p. 62 ; Min. 6471, 6551.
[2] A. III. Dig. p. 51 ; Min. 26308-29, 26435-52, 26462-8,

ment was doomed. It cannot be as tortfeasors that employers are held liable for the negligence of foremen whom they are paying to be careful. Their liability in cases of this kind can only be the liability of insurers. And, if employers are liable as insurers in one class of cases, why should they not be made liable as insurers in all ?

Such, in effect, is the general answer made by the workers to the employers' objections to their proposals. As has already been seen, however, they, as it were, throw a sop to Cerberus by adding : " After all, you will be able to throw all the burden upon the public. The employers' liability we want to extend would result in a tax, not upon profits, but upon production. Raise your prices in proportion and make the consumers pay you back." In taking up this position, the workers seek to justify themselves on three main grounds. First, that they have a claim upon the public, and that the principle of public insurance, whether against accidents, sickness, old age or starvation, is, and has already been acknowledged by the public itself to be, a matter of mere justice. Secondly, that the *salus populi* is so intimately bound up with their own, that it is to the public interest to incur the expense. And, thirdly, that a system of universal insurance would cause little or no additional expense, because it would make the employers, on whom it would primarily fall, more careful and minimise the number of accidents. And, in the words of Mr. G. Dew, representing the London Building Trades' Committee, " It is not that we want compensation ; it is that we don't want accidents."[1] The payment of compensation for negligence involves a large tax upon the public already. The payment of claims for insurance would probably not involve a larger, and it would certainly give rise to less of the litigation which transfers so much of the wealth of the nation into the pockets of the lawyers. In short, the principle of employers' liability, finding its logical conclusion in public insurance, is not "indefensible, novel and redundant," but equitable, admitted, and of great public utility.

Although a system of universal insurance against accidents is undoubtedly the aim of the workers, and though they have no objection to the employers shifting the burden on to the shoulders of the public, they, nevertheless, view their present practice of transferring their liability to the ordinary insurance companies with marked disfavour, and that, too, in full knowledge of the fact pointed out by several of the employers' representatives before the Commission that, without the aid of insurance companies, the smaller employers would never be able to pay any compensation at all. The men's representatives explained the apparent inconsistency by repeating their declaration that it was not compensation that they wanted. They wanted immunity. To put the liability upon the shoulders of the public in the form of higher prices serves merely to insure employers collectively against losses individually incurred, and so individuals still have a strong motive to be careful. But to put the liability upon the shoulders of

[1] C. II. Dig. p. 97 ; Min. 17425-9.

an insurance company serves to insure employers individually against those losses, and so tends to make
them individually careless. For, though their collective carefulness may affect the premiums they have
to pay, it is their individual carelessness that determines the compensation they receive. In fact, just as
life insurance is conducted on the principle of the
long-lived paying for the short, so accident insurance
is conducted on the principle of the careful paying
for the reckless. In the paramount interests of
safety, therefore,—so the workers argue—it should be
prohibited by law.

Again, insurance companies are wealthy corporations, conscious of no social relation with the workers,
and sticklers, in all cases, for their full legal rights.
A poor man has no chance against them in the law
courts. If the workman wins his case, they make
the employer appeal, and, if the appeal is dismissed,
appeal again, with the result that victory often proves
more expensive than defeat. Mr. J. Falvy, representing the South Side Labour Protection League,
gave a detailed account of some of the devices employed by insurance companies to prolong the course
of litigation when defending actions jointly with
employers, and said he considered that they should
be bound to satisfy the verdict if their clients were
defeated.[1]

Insurance against employers' liability was not to
be forbidden by the Bill of 1893. Section 4, however, contained a provision against a device adopted
by employers which was the subject of much greater

[1] B. I. Dig. p. 60 ; Min. 2770.

criticism on the part of the men's representatives
even than the practice of insurance. The device referred to is to persuade the men to "contract out,"
that is to say, to enter into an agreement whereby
they renounce the rights conferred on them by the
Act, and often also their common law rights, to be
indemnified for injury, the result of negligence. The
usual consideration given by the employers in entering upon a contract of this sort is a contribution to
the workmen's accident insurance fund, and the
evidence affords no instance of such a contract being
enforced without some consideration, other than that
of mere employment, being given by the employer.
At the same time, it is possible to detect a distinct
tendency towards making "contracting out" compulsory on mere consideration of employment. Mr.
Hodge, representing the British Steel Smelters'
Amalgamated Association, told of several attempts
to do so which had failed only owing to the efforts of
the Trade Unions,[1] and, in several cases where mutual
insurance funds exist, as, for example, among the
Lancashire miners and the employés of the London
and North - Western Railway Company, the state
of the case may be fairly described in the words of
Mr. G. G. Caldwell, a Lancashire coalowner, who
said, "membership of the fund is a necessary condition of employment, and members of the fund must
contract out of the Act."[2]

At present, it must be admitted, the practice of
"contracting out" has not resulted in any pecuniary

[1] A. II. Dig. p. 52 ; Min. 16429-33, 16572-8.
[2] A. I. Dig. p. 30 ; Min. 5927-8.

loss to the workmen. The employers in every trade where it prevails stated that the amount of their contributions to the funds was considerably in excess of the probable amount of the damages they would have to pay under the Act, and the men did not dispute the statement. On the contrary, they seemed, with few exceptions, to be very well satisfied with the compensation which the mutual insurance funds afforded them. In spite of this, it appeared to be the universal policy of the Trade Unions to prohibit "contracting out," and the universal policy of the employers to encourage it.

This matter of "contracting out," indeed, affords a good instance of the distinction that is often observable between the policy of the workmen and the policy of the Unions. The former looks almost exclusively to facts, the latter sometimes also to tendencies. The workman in his individual capacity is quite prepared to contract out of the Act as long as he gets a satisfactory *quid pro quo*. In his corporate capacity, he sees that, if he allows " contracting out " to become a universal rule, he is not likely to get a satisfactory *quid pro quo* very long. Thus, Mr. Caldwell told the Commission that his men preferred to contract out of the Act in order to obtain the benefits of the mutual insurance fund, but their Union, *i.e.*, the same men in their corporate capacity, disapproved of the practice. Accordingly, when a strike arose in 1881, the Union got its members out on a question of wages, and then added to the original demand a further one against " contracting out," which was not a grievance of which the men

complained.[1]   The case against "contracting out," in
short, is based, not so much upon its effects in the
present as appreciated by individuals, but upon its
effects in the future as foreseen by the Trade Unions.
The real ground of the opposition of the Trade
Unions to "contracting out," and the existence of
mutual insurance funds—for they are opposed to
both—is that they consider the policy of employers,
in supporting the funds at considerable immediate
pecuniary loss, to be directed against Trade Unionism itself.

Let us see how this contention is supported.   In the
first place, it was constructively admitted to be true
by the representatives of the employers themselves.
They all explained that their motive in incurring the
apparently gratuitous expense connected with the
funds, was " to acquire security for the continuance of
amicable relations between themselves and their
workmen."   In other words, the funds that served to
insure workmen against accidents, served also to insure employers against strikes.   In the second
chapter of this volume, it was pointed out how greatly
the creation of benefit funds assisted the Unions to
secure a hold over their members, and, in these mutual
insurance funds, the employers are practically fighting
the Unions with their own weapons.   The funds in
question can only flourish at the expense of the funds
of the Unions, for the workmen cannot and will not
support both so liberally as they would support
either of them independently.   And if the mutual
insurance funds, which furnish the sole excuse

[1] A. I. Dig. p. 30 ; Min. 6039-43.

for "contracting out," be themselves objectionable, how, it is argued, can the practice in question be defended at all ?

It can be defended on the ground that the end is superior to the means, and that, if the end, *viz.*, the good of the workman, be well served by the practice, arguments based on the interests of Trade Unionism, which is only one of the many means to that end, cannot be admitted. To this the Trade Unions reply that, if they are weakened, equal compensation may be paid for accidents now, but there will no longer be any guarantee that it will continue to be paid permanently, and, in any case, to weaken the Unions is to impair the machinery which alone can give the men other more 'important advantages, *viz.*, higher wages, shorter hours, etc. The interests of the workmen are ultimately identical with the interests of their Unions. If the Unions are weakened to-day, the workmen will lose it by to-morrow.

"Contracting out," moreover, is objected to on other grounds. As the men's representatives were never tired of insisting—"we don't want compensation, we want immunity"—and, like other systems of insurance, the payment of fixed annual contributions to a fund does not tend to make employers more careful. Very often, too, they tend to make the men themselves careless for the same reason ; but in one case—that, namely, of the Thames Ironworks Shipbuilding Company—this tendency is counteracted by the device of making the employer's contribution equivalent, not to those of the men, but to the amount

G

of the funds in hand at the end of the year after all claims have been met.[1]

And, finally, "contracting out" is objected to as a matter of principle. The Act is the workmen's charter, and all rights under it should be inalienable. An opinion to this effect was expressed, not only by the men's representatives, but also by Mr. J. E. Ludlow, the former Chief Registrar of Friendly Societies.[2]

The general policy of the workmen with regard to employers' liability, is a policy of extension. Some of the labour leaders, however, desired not to make employers liable as insurers, but rather to make more effective the old liability of the negligent person, be he employer, foreman, contractor, fellow-servant, or a member of the public, by treating the offence as criminal, and making it punishable by imprisonment. The adoption of this proposal would involve the surrender of compensation, but would, it was contended, make everybody more careful, and diminish the number of accidents, which is, after all, the paramount *desideratum*.

Evidence embodying this proposal was given by Mr. Keir Hardie, the late President of the Ayrshire Miners' Union, who said :—"At present, employers' liability does not affect the employers personally at all. They insure their risk under it with an insurance company, and charge the amount of their premiums to the working expenses of their firms. It is expedient, therefore, to substitute for the payment of a

---

[1] A. III. Dig. p. 44 ; Min. 24932-48, 25022-38, 25116-21, 27870-5.

[2] W. Dig. pp. 57, 58 ; Min. 1748, 1758-74, 1816-28, 1834-43.

money compensation a punitive sentence, as for a personal assault, and the burden should fall upon the person directly responsible, whether employer, manager, or fellow-servant."[1]

Mr. Davies, of the Amalgamated Society of Carpenters and Joiners, seemed to be hesitating between the two policies. While proposing to make employers insurers against accidents of all kinds, he added, "At the same time, I hold that the only just and lasting settlement of the question is to place the whole affair under the common law, even though it were to deprive the workman of the privilege he presently possesses of getting compensation for accidents resulting from the negligence of his fellow-servants. I do not want the workman to enjoy any peculiar advantage over the rest of the community."[2]

This concludes the review which it has been possible to obtain from the evidence of the present attitude of the workers with regard to the extent of employers' liability. Other subjects referred to by the witnesses were:—(*a*) The repeal of sections 3 and 4 of the Act of 1880, limiting the amount of damages recoverable, and specifying the period within which notice must be given of the injury, in respect of which the claim is made; (*b*) the limitation of the right of appeal from county courts to the High Court to cases in which a considerable sum of money is at stake; and (*c*) the provision of some administrative machinery to set the Act in motion.

If the Bill of 1893 had been passed, sections 3 and 4

---

[1] A. II. Dig. p. 29 ; Min. 13288-96, 13364-5.
[2] C. II. Dig. p. 99 ; Min. 18389-91, 18413, 18427.

of the Act of 1880 would have been repealed, and the right of appeal would have been limited to cases where the amount claimed exceeded £300. But no administrative machinery would have been provided. The proposals concerning this last point were:—(1) To allow either party to apply to a Government department to take up the case free of charge ; (2) to provide for regular and frequent inspection of staging, machinery, etc., likely to give rise to injury and so to litigation ; and (3) to appoint working men to Government inspectorships, with administrative powers under the Act.

These proposals appear to have been prompted mainly by a desire on the part of the Unions to avoid the expense which many of them are pledged to incur either by paying the costs of litigation under the Act, or by themselves providing accident benefit.

CHAPTER IV.

THE FACTORY ACTS, ETC.

Sanitation—Safety and Accidents—Coroner's Inquests—Tickets containing Particulars of Payment—Domestic Workshops and "Sweating"—Special Regulations for Special Processes —Overtime—Medical Certificates—Employment of Women —Employment of "Young Persons"—Employment of Children—Proposed Extensions of the Acts—Penalties— Administration—The Shop Hours Regulation Acts, 1886 and 1892.

MOST of the evidence taken before Committee C, and much of that taken before Committee A, of the Royal Commission on Labour, directly related to the text and administration of the Factory Acts, and upwards of 60 amendments were proposed by the witnesses.

Sanitation.—In some industries, the sanitary condition of factories was said to be bad; and, in almost all, the sanitary condition of workshops was said to be worse.[1] The fact was not attributed to any want

---

[1] The term "factory" is applied to all industrial establishments where manufacturing processes are carried on by the aid of mechanical "power," and to all establishments where certain specified processes are carried on, whether "power" is employed or not. All other manufacturing establishments are called "workshops."

of stringency in the provisions of the law, so much as
to the fact that its administration is entrusted to two
separate authorities, whose functions overlap and
whose relations are ill-defined. The inspectors under
the Factory Acts must prosecute occupiers who do
not keep their factories " in a cleanly state and free
from effluvia arising from any drain . . . or other
nuisance, or free from overcrowding while work is
carried on therein," or " ventilated in such a manner
as to render harmless, so far as is practicable, all the
gases, vapours, dust or other impurities generated in
the course of the manufacturing process or handicraft
carried on therein that may be injurious to health,"
but they have no power to order any structural alteration, and no power to prosecute for similar offences in
the case of workshops. Where structural alterations
are required, or where a workshop is concerned, they
must report the matter to the local sanitary authorities. And not only is there divided authority, but,
what is perhaps worse, divided responsibility. Under
the Factory Acts, the occupier is solely liable; but,
under section 36 of the Public Health Acts, a portion
of the liability is cast upon the owner; *i.e.,* " the
person receiving for the time being the rackrent of
the premises." Between the Factory Acts and the
Public Health Acts, between the Factory inspectors
and the local sanitary authorities, and between the
occupiers and the owners, there would seem to be so
much room for evasion that it is, on the whole, surprising that the law relating to the sanitary condition
of industrial establishments is even as well administered as it is,

This anomalous state of affairs has been the occasion of much legislative tinkering. Mr. J. H. Bignold, Her Majesty's Inspector of Factories in Devon and Cornwall, said that, up to 1872, the regulation of the sanitary condition of workshops was entirely in the hands of the local authorities; but they did nothing, and so it was entrusted to the factory inspectors; and now, in 1891, the local authorities are to have their powers restored, while "we are to keep them in check in some way—I don't know how."[1]

The reason why the local authorities had their powers restored, seems to have been that the factory inspectors were obviously overworked, and it was imperatively necessary either to relieve them of a portion of their duties, or to incur the expense of making a very large increase in the inspectorial staff. Most of the witnesses were agreed, however, in thinking that the system of dual control should be put an end to, and it was proposed to give factory inspectors entire control of this, as of all other matters affecting the internal arrangements of factories and workshops. It was pointed out that the inspectors were a more efficient and a more independent body of men than the local authorities, who, in many cases, owed their appointment to the local employers, whose delinquencies it was their duty to report. On the other hand, it was the opinion of some witnesses that the employment of the local authorities for this purpose was valuable, because sanitation was their speciality, and because their administration, being concentrated on a smaller area, was, therefore, more likely to adapt

[1] C. I. Dig. p. 62 ; Min. 10185-8.

itself to local requirements, besides admitting more
easily of that close and frequent attention which
sanitary affairs so imperatively demanded. A further
proposal was made by Mr. G. Keir, representing the
Amalgamated Society of Tailors, that Trade Union
officials, as well as factory and sanitary inspectors,
should be empowered to prosecute employers for
breach of the sanitary regulations.[1] But this was included in the more general proposal made by many of
the witnesses that " practical working-men," who
would be virtually the appointees of the Unions,
should be selected by Government to act in subordi-
nation to the factory inspectors, and assist them in
discharging all their multifarious functions.

It is noticeable that no proposal was made to put
an end to the dual liability of owners and occupiers
under the Public Health Act. On the contrary, Mr.
Sidney Webb, representing the Socialist movement,
desired to make owners of houses used for industrial
purposes share the occupiers' liability under the
Factory Acts as well.[2] This proposal, however, was
apparently not intended to relieve the occupier of any
part of his existing liability, but only to give the
prosecution two strings to its bow. Mr. Webb's idea
seemed to be to cast the *whole* liability both upon the
owner *and also* upon the occupier, *and also*, as will
be seen later in connection with domestic workshops,
upon the foreman or giver-out of work.

---

[1] C. II. Dig. p. 31; Min. 14669-92.
[2] W. Dig. p. 58 ; Min. 3747-8, 4413-7, 4437-40, 4453-67,
4507-27.

Safety and Accidents.—In regard to safety, the Acts are much simpler and more satisfactory; but, even in this respect, the inspectors have but little power in the case of workshops. As the law stands at present, the inspectors are authorised in the case of factories, but not of workshops, to see that all hoists, teagles, steam-engines, water-wheels, mill-gearing, and dangerous machinery, including driving-straps or bands, are securely fenced, and that "no child is allowed to clean any part of the machinery while the same is in motion by the aid of steam, water, or other mechanical power." The witnesses had no fault to find with these provisions so far as they went, but complained that they did not go far enough, and made the following proposals: First, that the use of shuttle-guards be enforced in textile factories; secondly, that the hours during which machinery should be stopped and cleaned should be specified; thirdly, that section 3 of the Act of 1878, which was repealed in 1891, should be re-enacted, but that the inspector should be authorised to prosecute immediately, instead of merely to send notice of default. The section in question related to the use of faulty grindstones, and read as follows:—" Where an inspector observes in a factory that any grindstone, worked by steam, water, or other mechanical power is in itself so faulty, or is fixed in so faulty a manner as to be likely to cause bodily injury to the grinder using the same, he shall serve on the occupier of the factory a notice requiring him to replace such faulty grindstone, or to properly fix the grindstone fixed in the faulty manner. . . . . . Where the occupier of a factory fails to keep the grindstone, mentioned in the notice, in such a state, and fixed in such a manner as not to be dangerous, the factory shall be deemed not to be kept in conformity with this Act;" fourthly, it was proposed to give the inspectors "power to deal" with the faulty construction of workshops; and, lastly, to extend their jurisdiction to all spars and planks used in the construction of staging in the boilermaking industry, and to all ropes and chains upon which such staging is suspended.

Coroners' Inquests.—It is provided by section 22 of the Act of 1891, that, in case of fatal accidents in factories or workshops, the following persons, namely, (*a*) the relatives of the deceased, (*b*) the factory inspector, (*c*) the employer, and (*d*) any person appointed by the order in writing of a majority of the workpeople employed in the factory or workshop where the fatal accident occurred, may attend the inquest and examine witnesses either personally or by counsel, solicitor, or other agent. The "persons appointed by the order in writing of a majority of the workpeople" are generally the Trade Union officials, and it was proposed to give them the right of attending whether definitely appointed to do so by the workpeople or not. It was further proposed to confine the composition of the coroners' juries to persons connected with the trade in which the fatal accident occurred.

In Scotland, there are, under ordinary circumstances, no public inquiries into the causes of fatal accidents. In the application of the Factory Acts to Scotland,

therefore, the following special provision is made:—
" Where a death has occurred by accident in any factory
or workshop, a public inquiry in open court shall be
held by the sheriff, upon the petition of any party
interested." It was the practically unanimous wish
of all the representatives of Scotch workmen that
this provision should be made unnecessary by a complete assimilation of Scotch to English law on the
subject of inquests.

Tickets Containing Particulars.—The Factory Act
of 1891, contains the following new clause :—" Every
person *who is engaged as a weaver* in the cotton,
worsted, or woollen, or linen, or jute trade, or as a
weaver or reeler in the cotton trade, and is paid by
the piece, in or in connection with any factory or
workshop, *shall have supplied to him with his work
sufficient particulars to enable him to ascertain the
rate of wages* at which he is entitled to be paid for
the work, and the occupier of the factory or workshop
shall supply him with such particulars accordingly."
Mr. A. Hopkinson, of the Bradford Warp Dressers'
Association, desired to insert the words, " or warp
dresser," after the word " weaver,"[1] and Mr. Arnold
Forster, representing the Bradford Chamber of Commerce, thought that to adopt this proposal " would
not interfere unreasonably with trade, and would
remove what might otherwise be a good ground of
complaint."[2] On the other hand, Mr. W. Noble, of
the United Cotton Manufacturers' Association, said:

[1] C. I. Dig. p. 66 ; Min. 5321.
[2] C. I. Dig. p. 66 ; Min. 6537-4.

—" I am still of opinion that this clause is a vexatious
and unnecessary interference with the private business
of manufacturers. . . . . They will be under the obligation to publish trade secrets.[1] The men's representatives were pleased with the clause, but thought
that it should be made more stringent by substituting.
the words, " full and express statement of the rate of
payment," for the words, " sufficient particulars to enable him to ascertain the rate of wages."

Domestic Workshops and Sweating.—Domestic workshops—that is to say, private houses, rooms or places,
where work is carried on solely by members of the
same family dwelling therein—are subject to Government regulation in respect of young persons of both
sexes under eighteen and children, but not in respect of
women. Some of the men's representatives proposed
to subject these places to the same regulations as workshops proper, but it was the general opinion that it
would never be possible to properly enforce any regulations in respect of them, whether of the Factory
Acts in the matter of hours, or of the Trade Unions
in the matter of wages. That this opinion is well-
grounded appears from the fact that it is in domestic
workshops that the evils known collectively as the
" sweating system " prevail ; for the term signifies
nothing more or less than *the employment of labour
in an industry where regulation exists under conditions in which such regulation is not enforced.* In
these circumstances, it is natural that the Trade Unions
should desire to abolish domestic workshops by com-

[1] C. I. Dig. p. 66 ; Min. 3968-9.

pelling employers to find work room on their own premises for all the hands they employ, and some of the witnesses proposed that a law to this effect should be passed immediately. The greater number, however, recognised that such a sudden change would have the effect of throwing many of the persons now employed in domestic workshops out of work altogether, and would not be viewed favourably by the great body of the workmen. The most generally accepted policy, therefore, was to accelerate the already observed tendency of domestic workshops to disappear by making it less worth an employer's while to support them, and it was accordingly proposed :—(a) To bring every place where two or more persons work in company, even if no wages pass between them, under the definition of a workshop proper; and (b) to make every giver-out of work responsible for the observance of the Factory Acts in whatever place he allows his work to be done ; and (c) to make all landlords responsible for the observance of the Factory Acts on the part of their tenants. If landlords wanted to free themselves from this obligation, they would be able to do so by inserting clauses in their leases to the effect that the houses were not to be used for industrial purposes, and it was contended that such clauses would probably be inserted with sufficient frequency to largely reduce the number of domestic workshops.

Special Regulations for Special Processes.—The evidence under this head may be briefly summarised as follows : — The employers' representatives complained of the stringency of the rules contained in the

Cotton Cloth Factories' Act, 1889, relating to "steaming" and the artificial production of humidity, and contended that the law should allow a similar latitude for "steaming" as for overtime. The men employed in red lead factories wished the special regulation of the Act of 1883, relating to white lead factories, to be applied to their industry. And the representatives of the Amalgamated Union of Bakers desired a law to be passed causing (*a*) underground bakeries to be prohibited; (*b*) all bakeries to be registered; (*c*) all bakeries to be built of white glazed brick; the object of the first and last proposals being to make baking more healthy, and of the second to make inspection more systematic.

Overtime.—The Factory Acts, while defining the period during which women, young persons and children may be employed, allow that period to be exceeded in certain cases. It was the opinion of the employers that the law should be made still more elastic, and, of the men, that it should be made absolute, the former contending that the statutory regulations were vexatious during periods of pressure, which should be utilised in order to counterbalance the periods of depression, and the latter, that if periodical pressure were made impossible, periodical depression would be impossible also. The opinion of the inspectors was divided on the subject, Mr. Bignold supporting the contention of the men,[1] and Mr. Henderson the contention of the employers.[2]

[1] C. I. Dig. p. 66 ; Min. 7309-10.
[2] C. I. Dig. p. 66 ; Min. 10105-8, 10120-3, 10153-66, 10194.

Medical Certificates of Fitness.—Section 27 of the Act of 1878 contains the following provision :—" *In a factory, a child or a young person* under the age of sixteen years shall not be employed for more than seven, or, if the certifying surgeon for the district resides more than three miles from the factory, thirteen work days, unless the occupier of the factory has obtained a certificate in the prescribed form of the fitness of such child or young person for employment in that factory." The proposals made by the witnesses were : First, that medical certificates should be required in *workshops* as well as in factories ; secondly, that they should be required for *women* as well as for young persons and children ; thirdly, that the medical examination of children should be periodical, and that, in that case, their certificates should not require renewing every time they changed their place of service ; fourthly, it was proposed to pay the certifying surgeons out of the public funds, just as the inspectors are paid, and thus to free them from all dependence on the mill-owners.

Employment of Women.—Most of the provisions of the Factory Acts, which we have so far dealt with, relate not so much to the persons as to the industrial environment of the women, young persons and children, whom they were designed to protect. The Acts, however, contain several sections which are personal to the workers, and, in the case of women, the most important of these is the 17th of the Act of 1891, which provides that " an occupier of a factory or workshop shall not knowingly allow a woman to be employed therein within four weeks after she has given birth to a child." The representatives of the Trade Unions in most of the industries where women are employed desired to extend the period during which mothers after confinement are excluded from factories from four weeks to six months, and some further proposed to exclude them for a stated period before confinement as well as after, while others went so far as to desire all married women to be excluded from factories altogether. The representatives of the nail-makers, moreover, wanted women to be forbidden to make nails larger than half an inch. All these proposals were frankly admitted to be based mainly upon a desire to get rid of the competition of female labour, which acted so prejudicially upon the men's wages and well-being. But they were defended on the ground that their adoption was imperatively demanded in the interests of the women themselves. It was, accordingly, contended that factory life was not only bad for the women's health, but interfered very greatly with their domestic duties, and that the loss of the mother's earnings would be compensated for by the increased earnings of the father, which would result from reducing the competition in the labour market. The first of these contentions was supported by Dr. J. Tatham, Medical Officer of Health for Manchester, who said :—" As a result of anxious inquiry extending over many years, I am convinced that very much of the excessive infant mortality in the town of Salford, where I acted as medical officer of health for fifteen years, is due to the employment of young mothers."[1]   The abolition of female labour was looked forward to by the workers generally as a desirable end in itself, but it was recognised to be impossible to suppress it without the aid of legislation, because poverty compelled individuals to support a system of which they collectively disapproved.   It was also recognised that a law suddenly abolishing female labour would, for the moment at any rate, increase that poverty, and so cause more evils than it would cure, and the general conclusion arrived at may be summed up in the words of Mr. Sidney Webb, who said that " it would be undesirable to definitely prohibit the employment of married women in factories and workshops . . . the proper policy is to hasten the advent of such a social development in which mothers of families should be released from their present necessity of working for their living."[2]

Employment of " Young Persons." — The term " young person " is defined as including all employés, whether male or female, " of the age of fourteen years, and under the age of eighteen years." With certain exceptions, they are subject to the same regulations as women with regard to hours of labour, etc., and may, roughly speaking, be said to correspond to " apprentices," a rank in the industrial army which is rapidly disappearing.   In some trades, however, such as the engineers', where the apprenticeship system still exists, the apprentices do not all come within the definition of " young persons " under the Factory

[1] C. I. Dig. p. 63 ; Min. 8141-4, 8152.
[2] W. Dig. p. 58 ; Min. 3747-8, 4437-40, 4453-67, 4507-27.

H

Acts, and employers are, accordingly, able to work them overtime in the same way as adult males, without paying them the same wages. There is, consequently, a perpetual struggle between the employers and the Unions, the former trying to overcrowd the trade with apprentices, and the latter trying to keep them out. In order to make apprentice labour less profitable, and less accessible to the employers, the representatives of the Amalgamated Society of Engineers desired to extend the definition of " young persons," so as to include almost all the apprentices, by raising the age to twenty-one. They feared, however, that this reform, consisting, as it would, merely in preventing apprentices being overworked, to the detriment both of themselves and of their seniors, might increase the existing over-popularity of the trade among lads starting in life, and considered that its adoption would oblige the Union to redouble its efforts to prevent too many apprentices being admitted. The witnesses, however, did not appear to desire any legislation on this point, but relied mainly upon "organising the apprentices already admitted, so as to make more effective the restraining influence they even now exercise upon lads desirous of entering the trade."[1] And a similar policy seemed to find favour with the representatives of the printing industry.

Employment of Children.—The term "child" is defined as meaning a person under the age of fourteen years. Under the Act of 1878, the employment of children under ten years of age is altogether prohibited

[1] A. III. Dig. p. 37 ; Min. 23234-61.

in a factory or workshop. The Act of 1891 has raised the age to eleven. The Scotch Education Act of 1883 requires, in addition, that all candidates for employment must pass the third standard, while the English Education Acts leave the determination of a standard to the authorities in the various districts. Child labour in factories is, therefore, permitted only in the case of those that have attained eleven years of age, and have passed a specified educational standard. And, even where these requirements are satisfied, it is permitted only subject to certain additional restrictions, which do not apply to women and " young persons." Of these, the chief are—(a) that children must either be employed only on alternate days, or only for half days; and (b) that children employed in factories or workshops must keep six school attendances a week.

The law on this point was the subject of much difference of opinion. Some of the men's representatives desired children to be altogether prohibited from working in factories and workshops till they reached the age of fourteen, while others considered that such prohibition would decrease the family earnings, and so entail greater hardships on the children than it would remove. Some of the employers supported the first, but most of them the second of these views. The opinions of the inspectors were equally divided. The only witnesses that were unanimous on the subject were the school teachers, who contended that the half-time employment of children during the progress of their school career was bad for them both educationally, physically, and morally. This contention, however, was contradicted by other witnesses, and seemed to have been chiefly motived by the disturbing effect of the half-time system upon the general school arrangements. Alternative proposals were, accordingly, made to the following effect :—(a) To merely raise the age at which children may be admitted to factories to twelve ; (b) to fix an educational standard instead of an age as the sole qualification for half-time work ; (c) to let such a standard be the fourth ; (d) to reduce the two methods, by which the school and factory hours of the children are dovetailed, to one ; (e) to provide separate schools for half-timers ; and (f) to prohibit the employment of children before 8 a.m. between 1st October and 31st March. But, of these, the first was the only one that received any large measure of support, and the second was met by a counter proposal to the effect that age and attendances should be the sole qualification for half-time work, and that such attendances should be the aggregate for the school career, instead of so many per annum. The general conclusion seemed to be that the abolition of child labour was desirable as an end in itself, but was inexpedient in many cases, and could only be usefully reached by slow degrees in most.

At the age of fourteen, a child becomes a "young person." He or she, however, can become a "young person" at the age of thirteen on passing a certain educational standard specified by the Home Secretary with the consent of the Education Department. The standard so specified for England is the fourth, and for Scotland the fifth ; but the Home Secretary allows the local authorities to fix a higher standard for the children within their jurisdiction. It was the opinion of Mr. W. H. Wilkinson of the Northern Counties Amalgamated Association of Weavers that the fourth standard was not sufficiently high [1]; and some of the other witnesses desired the sixth educational standard, instead of an age, to be made the sole qualification for the employment of children under fourteen as " young persons," while others considered that the sole quali- fication should be age and attendances. Very few witnesses, however, referred to the subject at all.

Proposed Extensions of the Acts.—At present, the Factory and Workshops Acts apply only to places where manufacturing work is performed by women, young persons, and children, and only in a limited degree to places where women, but not children, are employed, or where the work is carried on in a private house solely by members of the occupying family. It was, accordingly, proposed to extend them (*a*) to laundries where the work is not manufacturing work (*b*) to warehouses and dockyard work where women, young persons, and children are not employed, and (*c*) to places where women, but not children, are em- ployed, and where the work is performed in private houses, *i.e.*, domestic workshops, in the same degree as to other workshops. Laundries are mentioned for the first time in the Act of 1891, which empowers the Secretary of State to authorise the factory inspectors to report sanitary defects in laundries to the authori- ties under the Public Health Acts; but it is only in the matter of sanitation that occupiers of laundries are liable. The London Laundresses' Union recently got up an

[1] C. I. Dig. p. 63 ; Min. 1775.

agitation in favour of the extension of the Factory
Acts to the industry, and it appears from the report
of the Lady-Assistant Commissioners appointed to inquire into the employment of women, that the movement was viewed favourably by the larger employers
who could afford to keep a double staff, but was objected to by the smaller ones who were afraid that
they would lose their trade if they were obliged to
observe the limited and regular periods of employment
ordained by the Acts.   The proposal as to warehouses
and dockyards was made in the interests of safety,
and the proposal as to places where no children are
employed, and to domestic workshops, was made with
a view to the abolition of "sweating."

Penalties.—Under the Factory Acts, the occupier is
primâ facie responsible in all cases ; but, when charged
with an offence, he is permitted to summon any other
person whom he may charge as the actual offender, and
if he proves the charge, and also proves that he himself "has used due diligence to enforce the execution
of the Act," he can escape from his liability.   But he
must prove both these points.   Unless he can bring the
charge home to the actual offender, and also disprove
connivance on his own part, he remains responsible
for the breach of the Act.   It was pointed out by
some of the employers' representatives that, owing to
the stringency of these provisions, innocent employers
were often unable to get rid of their liability, and
suffered punishment accordingly, and that the law
ought to be modified in their favour.   As has already
been pointed out, moreover, it was also proposed to

make landlords and all givers-out of work share the employers' responsibility for the observance of the Acts.

Administration.—Owing to the large number and great variety of establishments subject to the Factory Acts, the task of administration is exceptionally difficult. At present, inspection is provided for by section 67 of the Act of 1878, which empowers the Secretary of State to appoint such inspectors as he may think necessary, subject to the approval of the Treasury as to numbers and salaries, but prohibits the appointment for this purpose of persons that are interested in factories or workshops, whether as occupiers or as workmen, or otherwise. In accordance with this section, there has been organised under the Home Secretary, a staff consisting of one chief inspector, four superintending inspectors, 40 district inspectors, and 20 junior inspectors, or 65 in all. In addition to this staff, two ladies have recently been appointed to assist the district inspectors in dealing with places where women are employed. The total annual appropriation for the Factory Department of the Home Office is about £31,000, of which about £5600 is devoted to the payment of inspectors' travelling expenses and other charges incidental to their work. The number of registered factories is 64,098, and of registered workshops 69,990, making a total of 134,088 establishments subject to Government inspection, excluding those not on the register.

Nearly all the witnesses concurred in thinking the present administrative machinery to be insufficient, and most of the complaints detailed above with

reference to sanitary and other defects were preferred
in support of this view. The deficiency of inspection
appeared to be specially marked in small towns, and
Mr. Davis, of the Irish National Bakers' Federation,
proposed that in these places the police should have
power to administer the Acts in default of the regular
inspectors.[1]

An increase in the staff was urgently demanded by
nearly all the witnesses, including the factory inspectors themselves. Most of the men's representatives pointed out that such an increase need not
involve such very great expense, because it would
most usefully be effected by appointing "practical
working men" at lower salaries and with lower qualifications than the regular inspectors, to act as assistants
to the members of the present staff. The advantages
of making such appointments were said to be—(a)
that men who possessed practical experience of factory
life would not be so easily hoodwinked as persons
taken from a superior class, and (b) that the sub-
inspectors would more easily gain the co-operation and
sympathy of the workers. The Acts, it was contended,
would be both better administered and more cheerfully
obeyed, if the workpeople felt that the Government
inspectors were virtually their own appointees. It
was also proposed to appoint a few sub-inspectors
from among the ranks of the female operatives, for
the benefit of the women whom the Acts were primarily intended to protect. And two witnesses, viz.,
Mr. W. Mosses, of the United Pattern Makers' Associa-

[1] C. III. Dig. p. 174 ; Min. 28847-50.

tion,[1] and Mr. J. Whittaker,[2] of the Amalgamated Society of Engineers, desired the inspectors to wear some badge by which they might be distinguished, the former witness adding that extracts from their reports should be affixed to the gate of every factory or workshop, in order that the workpeople might know that they were doing their duty. Finally, Mr. J. Henderson, the Superintending Inspector for Scotland and the North of England, said :—" I think it would be a useful aid to inspection if a popular publication of a few of the regulations were made, and if the inspector of each district were to appoint places of meeting where workpeople who desired information might come and apply for it."[3]

On the whole, therefore, there seemed to be a determined wish on the part of the workpeople to acquire greater control of the administrative machinery. In spite of this, however, it appeared from the evidence that they greatly neglected their duty of assisting the Government inspectors by calling their attention to defects. This neglect was excused on the ground that they were afraid of being " victimised" by the employers, and that they were often ignorant of the fact that communications to the authorities might be made anonymously. But the truth seemed to be that, though the workpeople, in their corporate capacity, approved of the Factory Acts, and desired them to be strictly enforced, yet, individually, they

[1] A. III. Dig. p. 32 ; Min. 20380-6, 22468-70, 22476-87, 22508-25.

[2] A. III. Dig. p. 91 ; Min. 22871-901.

[3] C. I. Dig. p. 68 ; Min. 8971-2.

were glad of the opportunity of breaking the law relating to overtime work, etc. The result was said to be
that they generally rendered their employers willing
assistance in hoodwinking the inspectors. In some
factories, they were said to have invented a regular
code of signals to warn one another of the inspector's
approach, and generally took care that, if there were
any irregularities, the inspector should never find
them out.

Evidence was also given concerning other matters
connected with the administration of the Acts. In
the first place, it was proposed to place the factory
and mining departments of the Home Office in an independent position, a proposal which was supported
by Mr. Henderson, the Superintending Inspector for
Scotland and the North of England,[1] or to attach them
to the newly established Labour Department, which, it
was contended, ought to comprehend all functions of
Government in relation to labour, whether administrative or statistical. Secondly, complaints were made
of the composition of the boards of magistrates, before
whom cases under the Factory Acts were tried. In
large manufacturing towns, they are composed almost
entirely of employers ; but, as was pointed out by Mr.
B. C. Wates, a partner in the firm of J. Whitmore &
Co., Worsted Spinners, Leicester, employers that are
scrupulous in complying with the Acts are only too
glad to get their rivals punished for not complying
with them.[2]   At the same time, it was generally considered among employers to be impolitic to sit on the

[1] C. I. Dig. p. 70 ; Min. 9082.
[2] C. II. Dig. p. 103 ; Min. 12649-51.

bench when cases came up affecting their own trade.
Thirdly, Mrs. Amie Hicks, representing the London
Ropemakers' Union, made a proposal to the effect that
employers under the Factory Acts should be obliged
to furnish balance sheets periodically to the Board of
Trade, which sheets should be used as indicating
what wages they could afford to pay. She did not,
however, desire the Government to settle what the
wages ought to be, but only to give publicity to the
balance sheets received.[1]   And, lastly, Messrs. C.
Booth[2] and Sidney Webb[3] said that something ought
to be done to make the registration of workshops
absolutely complete. This, they contended, would be
quite practicable if present arrangements were made a
little more systematic. The registration, said Mr.
Booth, should be simple and without charge, and
should not necessarily be preceded by an inspection.
The certificate should set forth, on the landlord's
authority, the amount of space occupied, the number
of persons employed, the nature of their occupation,
and such other particulars as the Acts required. It
should be in triplicate, one copy being for the landlord, one for the occupier, and one for the factory
department of the Home Office, and it should be
periodically renewed, and the landlord should be held
responsible for the registration being duly performed.[4]

[1] C. I. Dig. p. 70 ; Min. 8316, 8391-5.

[2] W. Dig. p. 58 ; Min. 5417-543, 5553-82, 5592-614, 5660-731,
5765-801.

[3] W. Dig. p. 58 ; Min. 3747-8, 4413-7, 4437-40, 4453-67,
4507-27.

[4] W. Dig. p. 58 ; Min. 5417-543, 5553-82, 5592-614, 5660-731,
5765-801.

The Shop Hours Regulation Acts 1886 *and* 1892.—
The Shop Hours Regulation Acts regulate the conduct
of distributive, just as the Factory Acts regulate the
conduct of manufacturing or productive establishments. Without giving a *précis* of their provisions,
it will perhaps be sufficient to briefly enumerate the
amendments suggested by the various witnesses.
These amendments were ten in number. They were:—
(*a*) To make the closing of shops in every town at a
fixed hour compulsory ; (*b*) to give local authorities
power to enforce any regulations for the closing of
shops which may receive the support of two-thirds of
the shopkeepers in any town or district; (*c*) to forbid employers to refuse references, except for a just
cause ; (*d*) to forbid shop assistants signing agreements not to take future situations within a certain
distance of their present situation ; (*e*) to establish a
fair rent court for shopkeepers ; (*f*) to require shop
assistants engaged in heavy work to have medical
certificates of fitness; (*g*) to insert, in a new Act enforcing early closing by local option, a provision as to
intervals for dinner and tea ; (*h*) to pass a resolution
urging local authorities to order the shops within their
jurisdiction to be closed at 7 p.m. on four, and at 9
p.m. or 10 p.m. on two days of the week; (*i*) to
state in the text of the Act the fund from which
municipal or county authorities are to pay the inspectors they " may appoint," under section 8 of the
Act of 1892 ; and (*k*) to empower the Home Secretary
to appoint special inspectors to administer the Acts.
The objects of these various proposals are sufficiently
obvious without any further comment or explanation.

They were, for the most part, viewed not unfavourably by the larger employers ; but the smaller shopkeepers complained that, if they were obliged to close
early, they would lose the patronage of the working-
men, for whom they chiefly catered.

CHAPTER V.

STATE AND MUNICIPAL EMPLOYMENT.

Governmental Employment as a Substitute for Private Employment — The Socialist Programme — Nationalisation of
Mines—Of Railways—Of Canals—Municipalisation of Land
—Of Water Supplies—Of Gas Supplies—Of Tramways—
Of Dwelling-houses—Of Hospitals—Of Docks—Of Factories
and Workshops—Municipalities and Contractors—Industrial Policy of State and Municipal Bodies.

THE extension of the direct industrial functions of
political bodies is advocated on two distinct grounds.
First, that employment by purely industrial firms is
inferior; and, secondly, that it is insufficient. An advocate of State and municipal employment, therefore, may be either a person who thinks it to be a
desirable substitute for private employment, or he
may be a person who thinks it to be an undesirable
substitute, but a desirable supplement. The first will
advocate it in the general interests of all workers, and
the second will advocate it only as a means of absorbing the unemployed. In the present chapter, it is
proposed to deal with State and municipal employment solely as a proposed substitute for private employment, and quite irrespectively of the question of

the unemployed, which will be dealt with in the chapter immediately following.

As has already been stated, to make the State the sole employer of labour, the sole landlord and the sole capitalist, is the ultimate goal of the Socialists. And, as a step towards the attainment of that goal, their representatives informed the Commission that they desired to organise all local industries under municipal and county authorities. But they distinctly disclaimed all idea of including complete municipalisation —still less complete nationalisation—of industry in their immediate political programme.

At the same time, they did venture to make certain definite proposals in the desired direction. Thus, they considered that the time had come when the State should enter into possession of all mines, with a view to entrusting their management to the County Councils and confiscating the mining royalties, and should buy out the railway and canal companies, with a view to managing them directly through a public department. They also considered that at any rate the larger and more wealthy municipalities should at once proceed to purchase the land in the towns and suburbs, for the purpose of letting small holdings to labourers, to buy out the water, gas, and tramway companies ; to build artisans' dwellings ; to entirely support and control the hospitals ; to purchase and administer all docks ; and to start factories and workshops for doing the work which they would otherwise give to contractors.

The proposal to the effect that the State should purchase the mines, confiscate the royalties and entrust

the control to the County Councils was made by
Messrs. W. Small [1] and J. Keir Hardie, representing
the Miners' Unions in Lanarkshire and Ayrshire
respectively. The latter gave the following account
of the method by which the reform should be effected :
—" No compensation should be paid to the royalty
owners, while the coalmasters should be paid, not the
total amount of the capital they claim to have sunk,
but only the actual working value of the colliery at
the time of its transfer. The State should step into
the position of the royalty owners, and the County
Councils into that of the coalmasters. The central
authority, indeed, would be too far removed to directly
administer all the mines of the country, and the
County Councils would, of course, place the pits
situated within their jurisdiction under the control of
experienced managers." [2]

Considerable light is thrown upon the bearings of
this proposal by the report of the Royal Commission
on Mining Royalties. From that Blue Book we
learn that, in the year 1568, the judges decided in the
case of the Queen v. Northumberland that only mines
of gold and silver belonged to the Crown, whereas the
baser minerals belonged to the owner of the estate in
which they were situated. But to the general rule
then laid down, there are, and always have been,
exceptions. The Crown, being, in theory, the ultimate landlord of the whole kingdom, still maintains
its rights over all minerals lying below the foreshore

---

[1] A. II. Dig. p. 25 ; Min. 10367-83.

[2] A. II. Dig. p. 28 ; Min. 12573-85, 12878-93, 12944-6,
12974-3042, 13048-9, 13412-5.

and inland waters, and, in virtue of certain Acts of Parliament, over all minerals found in the Isle of Man and other specified localities.

From this it is evident that the confiscation by the State of all mineral royalties bears a certain analogy to precedent, and its Socialist advocates made a great deal of the feudal theory of land tenure upon which the present rights of the Crown over minerals are based. Thus, Mr. Keir Hardie contended that the Crown, as representing the nation, really had a true legal as well as a moral right to the minerals as well as to the land already. That the law contradicted itself when it allowed individuals to claim rent and mineral royalties, while reserving for the Crown the absolute ownership of the soil. That neither law nor morality could justify the claims of individuals to monopolise what no individual had created.[1]

It was in accordance with these contentions that the Glasgow Trades' Council passed the following resolution :—" That this Council instruct the Secretary to state to the (Mining Royalties) Commission that it is in favour of mining royalties becoming national property, without compensation being given." Very few of the miners' representatives, however, except Mr. Keir Hardie himself, were in favour of such an extreme measure. Those who were in favour of the nationalisation of minerals, generally thought that the royalty owners ought to receive compensation, and, outside the Scotch districts, very few of them expressed themselves in favour of the nationalisation of minerals at all. If the royalties were to be

[1] A. II. Dig. p. 28.

I

abolished, they might think it desirable to relieve
the trade of so heavy a tax ; but, since it was
merely proposed to *transfer* them from one fund
to another, they did not see how the workers would
be benefited. To meet this objection, it was contended
that, if the mines and minerals became the property
of the State, and if the working of the mines were
entrusted by the State to the County Councils, the
workers would be able to get everything they wanted
by means of their political power, and also that the
wage fund would be increased in consequence of the
economy in working that would result from an
amalgamation of properties.   Mr. Small, moreover,
gave the Labour Commission some facts and figures,
which he had collected from an old sheet, to show the
superiority of the conditions of employment in the
seventeenth century when the mines of Scotland
were worked by the Government,[1] and Mr. Keir
Hardie insisted that the proposed reform " would give
to the community the £7,000,000 a year that now
forms the profits of the employers, as well as the
£8,000,000 now paid to the royalty owners, while the
workmen would be working for a master whose object
would be, not to make profits at the expense of the
lives of his operatives, but merely to supply the
demand for coal, and to secure a fair wage for those
engaged in its production."[2]   But, in spite of all these
arguments, the Socialists did not seem to have
inspired the miners as a class with any general desire

[1] A. II. Dig. p. 25 ; Min. 10382-3.
[2] A. II. Dig. p. 28 ; Min. 12573-85, 12878-93, 12944-6,
12974-3042, 13048-9, 13412-5.

to put the coalfields into the hands of a public authority, which would have the interests of other industries to consider equally with their own.

With reference to the State acquisition of railways, the following evidence was given by Messrs. Mann, Webb, and Hyndman. Mr. Mann said :—" It is expedient in the interests of the workers and the public, who control the Government, for negotiations to be opened without delay by the Board of Trade or some other department of State with the view of taking over the management of railways. Instead of consulting the interests of a body of shareholders, the public authority should aim both at making travelling as cheap as possible, and also at releasing railway employés from the long hours and other hardships which they are at present called upon to endure. The fact that the State railways in foreign countries compare, in some respects, unfavourably with those managed by private companies in this country, does not weaken the case in favour of public control, because, in those countries, public opinion is not sufficiently powerful to keep the industrial policy of the various Governments on the right lines."[1]

Mr. Webb's evidence was to a similar effect. He said :—" A desirable extension of the State's industrial functions would be the acquisition of railways, which are already subjected to a good deal of State regulation. They should be taken over by purchase under the Lands' Clauses Consolidation Act. Considerable portions of the German railway system have lately been taken over by the State, and both Government

[1] W. Dig. p. 17.

and nation are satisfied with the result. One great
advantage of such a change being adopted in this
country would be the opportunity of reducing the
excessive and criminal hours now worked by railway
employés. Where such hours are worked, the State
might fairly demand an abatement in the purchase
price, just as if it were taking over a house in a bad
sanitary condition. No harm would result from the
substitution of a single public monopoly for a number
of competing companies. A monopoly in private
hands is, no doubt, not so efficiently conducted as an
undertaking that has competitors to face, as is proved
by the comparative inferiority of the southern railways, where competition is slight, to the northern
railways, where it is severe, but the case of a monopoly
in the hands of the public authority is different."[1]

Mr. Hyndman, also, expressed himself as follows:—
"The first industry that the State should take over is
the railways. They are the great highways of the
country, but they have been converted by capitalist
Houses of Commons in the past from being worked in
the interests of the community to being worked in
those of shareholders and directors. The cost of the acquisition by the State of this vast property would probably amount to about £1,100,000,000, but the money
would be well spent. On becoming possessed of the
means of transport, the State should at once proceed
to reduce its cost. At present, the English railways
are managed far less economically than those of other
countries. The New York Central Railway, for example, compares very favourably in this respect with the

[1] W. Dig. p. 20 ; Min. 3794-801, 4181-200, 4640-55.

London and North-Western. During 1891, the average train loads on the former line were 250 tons, and the working expenses ·285d. per ton per mile ; whereas, on the latter, the average train loads were only 65 tons, while the working expenses amounted to ·658d. per ton per mile. Yet the New York Central Railway pays higher wages than the London and North-Western, and at the same time charges less than one-third as much for its fares." [1]

It was Mr. Hyndman, also, who proposed that the State should acquire the canals and manage the traffic, but he contented himself with the bare proposal, and did not support it by any special facts or arguments. [2]

The evidence of these three witnesses has been given at full length in order to do full justice to their very exhaustive and clear statement of their case. They spoke, however, on this point as individual exponents of the Socialist idea—not as representing the views of any determinate body of workmen. And throughout the evidence given by the representatives of the railway and canal workers, we look in vain for any confirmation of the opinions detailed above. The representatives of both industries were ready to welcome the interference of the State between themselves and their masters ; but the representatives of neither seemed anxious to let the State step into their masters' place. In this, as in all other matters, the worker would seem to refuse to allow his attention to be diverted by any à priori theories from the facts. His sole object is to get "more wages and less work."

[1] W. Dig. p. 23 ; Min. 8446-62 ; App. 150.
[2] W. Dig. p. 23 ; Min. 8446-62.

The Socialists may prove that State employment *ought* logically to enable him to get what he wants. But *will* it ? Or rather, since the State is already a very large employer of labour, *does* it ? A review of the large portion of the evidence that related to the employés of the Government will enable the reader to supply the answer.

Some of the evidence referred to was given by the Socialists themselves, and it is interesting to see how they approached a body of facts that seemed so directly to contradict their theory. Let us take Mr. Webb's evidence, for example, which is at once the most ingenious and the boldest. He said :—" One great practical advantage of placing industrial establishments under Government is that public criticism can more easily secure the remedy of evils in their administration, and the importance of maintaining this greater power of criticism is proved by the very existence of defects. Such a defect is the disregard paid by the Admiralty to the resolution of the House of Commons, in 1891, to the effect that all Government employés should be paid the wages current in the district, and the systematic non-recognition by Government officials of the men's Trade Unions. The labourers in the Deptford victualling yard are paid only from 17s. to 19s. a week, that is to say, exactly the same as the same class of labourers at Gosport and Devonport, where the cost of living is much less, while Mr. C. Booth classed all Londoners receiving less than 21s. per week, with families dependent on them, as being in poverty, and all those receiving less than 18s. a week regularly as being in chronic want. The present refusal of the Admiralty to recognise any person not employed in the yard as the representative of the Deptford labourers is a reversion to the policy which Trade Unions have been so long occupied in breaking down among private employers." [1]

Again, Mr. Quelch, another Socialist witness, said : —" Government employés ought, through their political power, to secure better conditions of labour than their fellows in private firms. Yet, only in a very few cases do the wages received by the workers in the Woolwich Arsenal compare favourably with those paid by private firms in the same locality. The labourers in the engineering shops near Woolwich, for example, get 24s. and 25s. per week. The Government defends the comparative smallness of its wages by pleading that its employés are guaranteed permanent employment; but the plea is not valid, since Government hands are equally subject to dismissal with other workmen. At Woolwich, moreover, the house rents—10s. per week for a small house, and 12s. for one of six rooms, in both cases including rates, taxes and water, but excluding gas—are as high as they are in London." [2]

The Government employés themselves complained chiefly of the exceptional difficulty which they had in bringing pressure to bear upon their employer. It is true that they have the political power of which the Socialists made so much ; but this, they contended, does not compensate them for the relative

[1] W. Dig. p. 20 ; Min. 3779-93, 4045-6, 4477-9, 4505.
[2] A. III. Dig. p. 56; Min. 23727-34, 23763-5, 23787-91, 23837-48, 23907-16.

weakness of their Trade Union power. It has already been seen how Trade Unions owe their effectiveness to the employers' fear of strikes. And the Government has no fear of strikes. As was pointed out by Mr. Gould, a shipwright employed in the Portsmouth dockyard, " it would be futile to strike against the powerful arm of the Government,"[1] which, if its industrial undertakings fail, has the taxes to fall back upon. The Government, moreover, can only be approached through the officials, and officialdom, with its fixed and regular salaries, cannot be frightened.

A large number of complaints were also made concerning the low wages and general inferiority of the conditions of labour in Government establishments; but, as the financial secretary to the Admiralty pointed out, there were compensating advantages,[2] and, according to Mr. Ben Tillett, the alleged inferiority applied to the condition of the artisans, rather than to that of the unskilled labourers in whom he was chiefly interested.[3] Fortunately, therefore, for the Socialists' contention as to the intrinsic superiority of State employment, the charges which they themselves assisted in making against the Government cannot be said to be fully substantiated. But whether the grievances of Government employés be greater or less than those of their fellows in private employment, it seems clear that the machinery which they possess for securing redress is inferior,

[1] A. III. Dig. p. 57 ; Min. 21750, 21955-67.
[2] A. III. Dig. p. 62.
[3] B. I. Dig. p. 17 ; Min. 3991-2.

for their Unionism is necessarily weak, and their compensating political pressure to be effective must be backed by the political pressure of other persons as well.

Of course the Socialists would reply that, if State employment were universal, the political pressure of the Government employés would be overwhelming; but this argument is based upon the assumption that the interests of labourers of all classes are always identical, whereas, as a matter of fact, they are often conflicting. The whole policy of the miners, for example, is the aggrandisement of their trade at the expense of all the rest. And, in the shipbuilding industry, to which Government employment already largely extends, we learn from the evidence of all its representatives that by far the largest number of strikes arise out of disputes among members of the several trades as to the demarcation of work. It is not surprising, therefore, that the members of these trades, at any rate, should not highly value the political pressure which they can apply only with the co-operation of their rivals.

It is now time to turn to the proposals as to municipalisation, and here we shall find a much stronger *consensus* of opinion between the workmen and the Socialists. First, it was proposed to extend the municipal ownership and administration of land. In this connection, Mr. Mann said that " Parliament should show a readiness to grant the petitions of County and Town Councils for power to obtain land from owners at a fair price, to be let out at fair terms as small holdings to labourers." [1] Mr. Webb, moreover,

[1] W. Dig. p. 17.

said that "it was, generally speaking, desirable for a
municipality to purchase land whenever it was
practicable. In the case of London, though it would
probably pay to purchase the site of the metropolis at
present prices in view of a probable rise in its value,
it would be better to tax the ground landlords before
buying them out, and, by raising the rates, perhaps,
eventually to 20s. in the £, to reduce rents, and so
depreciate the property."[1] Mr. Webb also expressed
approval of a proposal made by Mr. Haldane, Q.C., to
the effect that the land in question should be valued,
and the London County Council be empowered to
take it over at any future date at its value to-day,
plus compensation to the owners for improvement.
This proposal, he contended, was just, for, inasmuch as
any rise in the unearned increment would be caused
by the community, the community would have a perfect right to intercept it.[2] In opposition to this argument concerning the much discussed "betterment"
principle, Sir Thomas (now Lord) Farrer, a member of
the London County Council, and an anti-Socialist,
quoted the expressed opinion of Lord Hobhouse, who
is chairman of the committee entrusted with the administration of such landed property as the Council
already possesses, that "the less of that kind of property the Council had to manage the better."[3] The
workmen's representatives did not as a rule refer to
this matter, because it has no direct connection with

---

[1] W. Dig. p. 20 ; Min. 3630-54, 3667-96, 3852-62, 3886-900,
4019-32.

[2] W. Dig. p. 20.

[3] W. Dig. p. 24 ; Min. 7939.

any particular trade. The dockers' representatives, however, expressed themselves in favour of the municipalisation of land in the neighbourhood of the docks, the cultivation of which would—so it was contended—relieve the men from their present absolute dependence upon their precarious calling, and there was nothing in the evidence given by the representatives of other trades to show that the proposed reform would be distasteful to them.

Municipal ownership and administration of water supplies was advocated by Messrs. Mann[1] and Webb as being a practicable immediate reform. The latter further expressed his opinion that the municipalities should supply the water without charge to the consumers, and pointed out that, even at the present time, there was communism with regard to water, inasmuch as every man used it according to his pleasure, and paid for it according to his means.[2]

Municipal ownership and administration of gas supplies also was advocated by the same witnesses, and by Mr. Thorne, representing the Gas Workers' and General Labourers' Union.[3] In this case, however, Mr. Webb doubted whether it would be expedient to allow consumers to use as much as they pleased irrespectively of their payments, although he considered that the gain resulting from the abolition of the present costly system of measuring would certainly be great. He pointed out, moreover, that in no single

[1] W. Dig. p. 17.
[2] W. Dig. p. 20 ; Min. 3863.
[3] C. III. Dig. p. 34 ; Min. 25111-21, 25314-8, 25374-9, 25390-401,

case where gasworks had passed under the municipalities in England had it ever been seriously proposed to follow the example of Philadelphia, U.S.A.,
and hand them over again to a private company.[1]

Mr. Webb also advocated the municipal ownership
and administration of tramways. In certain circumstances, he thought, they ought to run free of charge·
Indeed, he considered it probable that the difficult
problem of housing the poor of our cities would never
be solved without a very liberal service of free public
tramways between the centre and the suburbs.[2] In the
town of Huddersfield, where the tramways have been
worked by the corporation for the last twelve years, it
appears from the evidence of Mr. J. Pogson, the
manager of the tramways in question, that the experiment has not yet resulted in a financial success ; but
he pointed out that " the loss did not seem to concern
the ratepayers of Huddersfield. There was no desire
to lease the undertaking, and no company would get
the tramways with the good-will of the corporation
or the community." [3]   Mr. Tom Walker, moreover,
representing the Huddersfield tramway employés, said
that he considered it to be " a great advantage, from
the point of view of the men, that these undertakings
should be the concern of the local authorities, instead of being worked under a company." [4]   The
municipalisation of tramways was also advocated by
all the representatives of tramway workers examined

[1] W. Dig. p. 20 ; Min. 3864, 4539-91.
[2] W. Dig. pp. 20, 21 ; Min. 3865-8.
[3] B. III. Dig. p. 26 ; Min. 18903-4, 18907-9.
[4] B. III. Dig. p. 25 ; Min. 18683-6, 18700-5.

before the Commission, and one of them, *viz.*, Mr. G.
T. Jackson, of the Northern Counties Amalgamated
Tramways and Hackney Carriage Employés' Association, went so far as to say that Parliament should
prohibit municipal authorities from granting a lease
of their tram lines to companies, and should thus compel them, in all cases, to work their trams themselves.[1]

Municipal ownership and administration of artisans'
dwellings was advocated by Mr. Webb, who contended
that they should be provided at an improved quality,
rather than at reduced rents, inasmuch as the benefit
of any such reduction would probably be intercepted
in the form of reduced wages by the tenants' employers.[2]   As a commentary, moreover, upon this proposal, the evidence of Mr. Shepherd, of the Barrow-
in-Furness Dock Labourers' Union, may be cited, who
said : " The Barrow Corporation has not put into
operation its powers under the Artisans' Dwellings Act,
because it wants rents to be higher."[3]   Mr. Webb also
considered that municipal ownership and administration ought to be extended to hospitals.   " These institutions," he urged, "are already supported mainly out
of the rates, and, inasmuch as private subscription is
a very objectionable mode of maintaining public services, they should be supported out of the public funds
entirely."[4]   Mr. Giffen, moreover, the permanent
official at the head of the new Labour Department,

[1] B. III. Dig. p. 19 ; Min. 17908-13, 17969-73.
[2] W. Dig. pp. 20, 21 ; Min. 3865-8.
[3] B. II. Dig. p. 22 ; Min. 13558-61.
[4] W. Dig. p. 21 ; Min. 3872-4, 3882-5.

so far supported Mr. Webb on this point as to say that the application of State action and expenditure to the control and endowment of public hospitals would be more beneficial than the application of the same forces to insurance against accidents and old age.[1]

It is now necessary to attempt to summarise the large mass of evidence relating to the municipalisation of docks. This was advocated by Messrs. Mann and Tillett, and most of the representatives of the Dockers' Union, with special reference to the docks of London. On this point, Mr. Webb was not quite in agreement with his fellow Socialists, for, while approving of the municipalisation of docks as a matter of general principle, in the particular case of London he thought it would be better to entrust the management to a body like the Mersey Docks and Harbour Trust than to a committee of the London County Council, because bodies outside the county of London, such as the municipality of West Ham, were concerned,[2] and, in this, he was supported by the representatives of the various dock companies. As to the desirability of concentrating all the London docks under one control of some sort or other, however, nearly all the witnesses were agreed, although many of them doubted whether it would be practicable.

Mr. Mann came forward with a definite proposal, with the view of reforming the London docks, which was the subject of a great deal of criticism, and which may be shortly detailed as follows:—First, for the Government to hold a public inquiry into the present

[1] W. Dig. p. 43 ; Min. 7014-28.
[2] W. Dig. p. 21 ; Min. 3872-81, 4002-18, 4342-5.

administration of the port of London and the relations of that port with its competitors, both at home and abroad. Secondly, for the London County Council, furnished with the knowledge afforded by that inquiry, to apply to Parliament for power to take over the docks by compulsory purchase, and to borrow the necessary funds. Thirdly, for the Council, on entering into possession of the property, to put into execution a vast engineering scheme, drawn up by Mr. Mann himself, and approved of by a leading engineer, who estimated the cost at £6,684,000, excluding the purchase of the land. The effect of the execution of this vast work was explained by Mr. Mann to be to bring the docks nearer together, and nearer to the centre of distribution, thereby obviating nineteen twentieths of the work of reloading into trucks and lighters, and so enabling the work of the port to be performed with 7000 fewer men than are at present required, and 11,000 fewer than are at present hanging about the docks. And, fourthly, for the Council to cause its dock employés to be registered, and to give all the men on the register permanent employment and a complete monopoly of the work.[1]

In connection with this scheme, Mr. Mann stated that municipalisation was desired in order to make employment more regular, and that the Council would not be able to make employment more regular unless the dock area were made more compact. Topographical conditions, he argued, make it impossible to carry on the work of the port unless each dock is surrounded by sufficient men to meet its

[1] W. Dig. pp. 18, 19 ; Min. 2129-240.

maximum individual requirements. Mr. C. Booth
suggested that the difficulty might be got over by
affording information as to vacancies and facility of
transit from dock to dock ;[1] but Mr. Mann contended
that this suggestion was valueless, because it pre-
supposed three impossible conditions:—First, an agreement to be made on the point among the various
employers, of whom some are individuals, some companies, some sub-contractors, and some gangs of
men, but no one of whom poses as a philanthropic
body, or is likely to countenance concerted action.
Secondly, a fund for the payment of the cost of
transit from dock to dock.   And, thirdly, an oblitera-
tion of the feelings of resentment with which a workman from a strange dock is regarded by both employers and employed.[2]

Mr. Mann's own scheme was criticised by Colonel
Birt, the General Manager of the Millwall Dock Company, in the following terms:—" A scheme for the
concentration of the London docks might have good
results ; but only if it were possible to localise them
in the neighbourhood of London Bridge, where both
the price of the land—about £200,000 an acre in that
quarter—and the shallowness of the water prove in-
superable obstacles.   And if they were to be situated
at a point accessible to the large steamers, the small
vessels would lose the monopoly they now enjoy, while
the cost of lighterage would not be materially diminished by merely shortening the distance between the
centre of distribution and the docks.   Of course, if it

---

[1] B. II. Dig. p. 8; Min. 11373-82.
[2] W. Dig. pp. 18, 19.

were possible to discharge the cargoes from all vessels immediately alongside the warehouses, a certain advantage would be gained. But it is not possible— in the first place, because there is not and could not ever be sufficient room, and, in the second, because a ship's cargo very often consists of several classes of goods, each of which ought to be warehoused separately, and merchants insist on warehousing their goods in the City."[1]

Sir Thomas Farrer, moreover, made the following remarks:—"Mr. Mann's proposal is open to many grave objections. Apart from the engineering and financial difficulties of the scheme, which appear to be very great, its adoption would, on Mr. Mann's own admission, involve the discharge of about 1200 men. Furthermore, whether compensation be paid for the displacement of the existing docks, or not, the capital invested in them would in either case be wasted. Again, the scheme would increase the local congestion of street traffic in the neighbourhood of the new docks, and would necessitate the making of new thoroughfares to relieve it. The dangers of navigation, moreover, would be intensified by bringing the large steamers up so high. And, finally, it is very doubtful whether the County Council would manage the docks so well as the existing authorities. For years there has been a constant struggle to transfer docks, harbours, etc., from the hands of the municipalities to those of dock and harbour trusts, or other bodies representing the trade, because the former used to make use of their control

---

[1] B. I. Dig. p. 27 ; Min. 7019-53.

K

of the highways of commerce to tax the trade of the
country for the benefit of their own ratepayers."[1]

The last item in the collectivist programme, as pre-
sented to the Commission, was the establishment by
municipal bodies of factories and workshops, etc., for
the performance of their own productive work, instead
of giving it out to contractors. According to Messrs.
Mann[2] and Webb,[3] the first step in this direction
should be for municipalities to manufacture clothes for
the use of their own servants, the latter pointing out
that this reform stood on a different footing from the
rest, in that it involved the principle of opening new
businesses, instead of merely acquiring businesses
started by others. This proposal was criticised by Sir
Thomas Farrer at some length. He said: "While
there is no doubt that a public body is placed at a dis-
advantage as compared with a private individual in
dealing with its contractors, inasmuch as any subsequent modification of the contract is made the subject
of criticism and suspicion, yet the dangers and
difficulties attending the alternative plan of the public
body undertaking the direct conduct of its work are
far greater and more numerous. In cases where
machine work is a large element of the cost, all the
conditions that make the intervention of the contractor
beneficial are present. There must be an adequate
superintending staff and a sufficient body of permanent
foremen, and on their efficiency the success of the
application of the machine labour and the satisfactory

---

[1] W. Dig. p. 24 ; Min. 7904-8.

[2] W. Dig. p. 17.

[3] W. Dig. p. 21 ; Min. 4617-39.

execution of the work must depend. There will, therefore, be small room for saving the contractor's profit, for adequate industrial prizes in the shape of high reward and remuneration must be given to the staff, if the best men are to be secured in competition with analogous private enterprise. Again, there must be adequate plant and suitable buildings suitably situated. That plant must be adequately and regularly employed so as to be up to date and in the highest efficiency, and it must be renewed and replaced so as to be in line with every improvement and every fresh substitution of machine for hand labour which is the chief characteristic of modern production. Probably in ten years, the most modern and costly plant, and the most advanced and enthusiastic staff would have dropped hopelessly behind in the industrial struggle, if devoted to employment by public bodies and upon public work. Where hand labour, moreover, is the leading element of cost, the system of contracting is equally advantageous. Hand labour furnishes great room for misapplication and waste of energy, and for variation in the quality of the work. It is, therefore, universally found to require exceptional care in organisation and control, and such care cannot be reasonably looked for where no adequate interest is involved in its exercise. The contractor stands to lose as well as to win; but the public body does not. Its officials and workmen are alike aware of this, and regulate their conduct accordingly." [1]

In fact, the gist of Sir Thomas Farrer's argument would seem to be that the public authority would

[1] W. Dig. pp. 24, 25 ; Min. 7770-4.

furnish less employment relatively to the funds at
its disposal by undertaking the work itself than by
letting it out to contractors whose management would
be much more economical.

Very little evidence was given on this subject by
the representatives of the Trade Unions. Those that
did mention the subject of public contracts, however,
complained that they were cut so miserably fine that
the contractors were obliged, in self-defence, to
"sweat" their hands. In so far, therefore, as disapproval of the conditions of employment by public
contractors is evidence of approval of direct employment by the municipalities themselves, the Trade
Unions may be said to have supported the Socialist
proposals. In most cases, however, the more approved
policy was to compel the municipalities to insert the
"fair wages clause" in their contracts.

The Socialist witnesses accompanied the above
proposals with the following suggestions as to the
policy which the municipalities should adopt with regard to their industrial undertakings. To obtain the
necessary funds, it was suggested that they should increase the burden of rates on the owners of real
property, and raise loans on the security that the
rates afforded. In regard to their employés, it was
urged that they should keep their wages slightly in
advance of those paid by the best paying firm in the
same line of business in the town, a policy which, it
was contended, should be easy for them, because, having
the rates at their back, they would be relieved from
the necessity of making profits. They should also
endeavour always to arrange their work in such a way

as to dovetail with the experienced irregularity of employment under private firms, and even go so far as to anticipate future work in order to provide employment for those out of work at present. They should also devote a large portion of what profits they might make to providing capital for undertaking fresh industrial enterprises, with a view to ultimately becoming both proprietors and managers of all the engines of production within the limits of their jurisdiction. This policy, as embodied in many of the recent acts of the London County Council, was made the subject of severe condemnation by Sir Thomas Farrer, who contended that " it was not only unjust to the ratepayers, but was one which, if adopted by a private firm, would soon result in bankruptcy. Its main feature," he added, " is an attempt to raise wages artificially in defiance of the fact that both wages and profits must ultimately be paid out of the produce, and that it is only by increasing production that wages can be permanently and universally raised. It is impossible to divide a shilling amongst twelve men in such a way as to give 2d. to each."[1]

[1] W. Dig. p. 25 ; Min. 7775-83.

CHAPTER VI.

THE UNEMPLOYED.

How can Vacancies be more easily discovered?—Labour Bureaux—The Chelsea Employment Bureau—A proposed National Central Labour Bureau—How can Vacancies be multiplied in existing Establishments—State Regulation of the Hours of Labour—The Resuscitation of Agriculture— Emigration—Prohibition of Pauper Immigration—How can Employment be provided in default of Vacancies in existing Establishments?—Relief Works—Labour Colonies— Artificial Employment and Poor Law Reform—How can Relief be given in default of Employment?—Old Age Pensions—Mr. C. Booth's Scheme—Mr. Loch's Criticism— Opinion of Mr. Giffen.

WHATEVER view may be held as to the respective merits of employment by political and by purely industrial bodies, it may still be argued that State and Municipal employment are better than no employment at all. And it is a matter of common knowledge that a large number of persons are necessarily thrown out of work during the periodical periods of depression that seem to be an inevitable incident of the modern industrial system. The problem of the unemployed, however, involves too many issues to be treated merely as an appendage to the question of public employment, and the evidence relating to it must be summarised according to a fresh scheme, in

150

which the expediency of governmental provision of work for the workless will be discussed in its proper place.

Inability to get work may be due to two different causes. Sometimes it can be traced merely to imperfect means of communication between men wanting work and employers wanting men. Thus, an employer may be unable to get a vacancy adequately filled when the very man for the post is wandering about in vain search of a market for his services· Sometimes it arises from the fact that there are literally not enough vacancies to absorb the candidates for employment. And this absence of vacancies may be attributed sometimes to the failure of employers to engage so many hands as they might, sometimes to an insufficiency of industrial establishments, and sometimes to the incompetency of the persons seeking work. The solution of the problem, therefore, depends upon finding a satisfactory answer to four distinct questions:—First, can vacancies be more easily discovered ? Secondly, can vacancies be multiplied in existing establishments ? Thirdly, can work be provided in default of vacancies in existing establishments ? And, fourthly, can relief be given in default of work ?

The secretary to the Labour Commission informs us in his Memorandum on the Rules of Associations that various regulations have been adopted by the Trade Unions with a view to solving the first of these questions. " In many," he writes, " a register is kept of the names and addresses of members who are out of work. This is called the ' vacant,' ' out of work,'

'call,' or 'job' book or slate, and it must be signed
every day, or, in some cases, once or twice in each
week, by members who are in want of employment.
By means of such registers, employers can obtain information with regard to the number of men at their
disposal, and the Trade Union officials are enabled to
exercise some supervision over the unemployed members, and to satisfy themselves that the recipients of
benefit are honestly endeavouring to find work. When
a vacancy comes to the knowledge of the secretary, he
offers it to the member whose name stands first on
the list, and if this member refuses it without sufficient cause he is often suspended from benefit for a
time, or is obliged to place his name last on the list.
Employers are, however, as a rule, allowed to ask for
any particular man by name, and if the man thus
called for is not the first on the list, he has the option
of refusing to take the work. When members obtain
employment they are required to cross off their names
in the 'vacant' book within a stated period, or are
subject to a fine. In several societies, a list of shops
where men are wanted, is kept at the office for the
use of the unemployed members, and the secretary of
each branch is required to give all the information in
his power with regard to vacancies to unemployed
members of his branch, or those of other branches
who are travelling in search of work. All members
are urged to give information at once to the secretary
of their branch of any vacant situation of which they
may have knowledge ; and, in some societies, e.g. the
Dundee Branch of the United Journeymen Brass-
founders' Association of Great Britain and Ireland, a

fine is imposed upon members who neglect to do so within twenty-four hours. A few societies, such as the Durham County Colliery Engineers' Mutual Aid Association, forbid their unemployed members to apply for any situation without first informing the branch secretary of their intention. In the larger societies, *e.g.* the Amalgamated Society of Engineers, the secretary of each branch is required to send a report of the number of unemployed members and of vacant situations in the neighbourhood to the central office once in every month or quarter, and upon these returns the general secretary bases a report of the condition of the trade in the various districts, which is published periodically. When it appears from such reports that there is an opening for more labour in any district, the secretary can generally direct the removal there of unemployed members from other districts, and part or the whole of their fares are in such cases paid by the society. In some cases, moreover, the societies pay the fares of members who have obtained work at a distance, although, in some instances, repayment is necessary within a fixed period."[1]

Apart from the Trade Unions, who, as was pointed out by Mr. John Burns,[2] in the *Nineteenth Century* for December, 1892, are, above all things, anxious to get their unemployed members off their hands, agencies for finding employment have been established

---

[1] Rules of Associations, *Introd.*

[2] Mr. John Burns, being unable to attend when called upon to give evidence, forwarded the article referred to, in order to acquaint the Commission with his views.

under the name of labour bureaux or free labour registries. They are conducted on philanthropic, rather than commercial principles—that is to say, the object of their promoters is not so much to make a profit, as to bring employers and workmen together, and, though in some cases a fee is charged, they are barely and rarely self-supporting. Mr. W. H. Gardener[1] and the Rev. W. Tozer[2] furnished full particulars of the bureaux established at Egham and Ipswich respectively, and Mr. Scammell,[3] the honorary secretary of the Exeter and District Chamber of Commerce, put in evidence certain documents relating to the bureaux conducted by the Young Men's Christian Association, the Regent Street Polytechnic Institution, and the Salvation Army.

All these witnesses, however, while speaking in enthusiastic terms of the good work their bureaux were doing, were very anxious that they should be taken off their hands. As has been already stated, they none of them pay their way, and the task of managing them, though praiseworthy, is necessarily a very thankless one. Not only can no money be made out of them, but, as the witnesses pointed out, their promoters are in constant danger of offending the Trade Unions by unwittingly supplying " blacklegs " to employers during strikes, etc. It was, accordingly, contended that they should be taken over by the municipalities, and their expenses defrayed out of the rates. " Working men," said Mr. Tozer, " will not put

---

[1] W. Dig. p. 27.

[2] W. Dig. p. 28.

[3] W. Dig. p. 29.

confidence in institutions worked by capitalists or
employers, and employers will not put confidence in
institutions governed by Trade Unions. The bureaux
ought, therefore, to be entirely removed from the
area of both influences, and be placed upon a public
basis." [1]

An object lesson in the form of municipal action
here suggested is furnished in the case of the bureau
which was established by the Chelsea Vestry, in September, 1891. Mr. T. Smyth, whose election to the
office of its superintendent had been secured by the
support of the Trade Unions, fully explained its
operations, and stated that it was largely appreciated
and utilised by both employers and employed.[2] The
chairman of the Finance Committee of the Chelsea
Vestry, however, in his report for 1892, criticised the
Labour Bureau in somewhat severe language. He said
that it had failed to perform the services expected of
it, and was too costly in proportion to the number of
persons for whom it found employment. He pointed
out that the largest class of engagements was that of
charwomen and domestic servants, who could obtain
free registration at the ordinary servants' registry
offices, and he contended that the bureau offered no
proof that the larger proportion of persons whom it
sent to places really engaged themselves, or that their
engagements were permanent, while the number of
bonâ-fide male workers for whom employment of any
kind was found was only 2·5 *per diem.* He also
criticised the various figures, with the object of show-

[1] W. Dig. pp. 28, 29 ; Min. 6227-31.
[2] W. Dig. p. 28.

ing that every person sent after a place had cost the vestry over 2s.

This unfavourable report was quoted by Mr. Loch, the secretary of the Charity Organisation Society, in support of his contention that labour bureaux were practically useless. "The experience of the society," he added, "has not been in their favour, and there was a strong body of opinion among the witnesses examined by a special committee of the society that sat last year to inquire into homeless cases, to the effect that they have tended to demoralise the men, by causing them to relax their efforts both in seeking work for themselves, and in sticking to the work found for them" (a fact, by the way, which Mr. Tozer disputed). "Labour Bureaux," Mr. Loch continued, "are generally formed when employment is scarce, and it is precisely during such times that they are useless, for employment cannot be discovered by a bureau when there is no employment to be found." [1]

It may be at once objected that this argument is far too sweeping. The fact that the bureaux would be useless, if there were absolutely no vacancies to be discovered, does not prove them to be useless for the purpose of discovering what vacancies there may be, when employment is merely scarce. One might just as well argue that, because it is useless to dig for gold where there is none, therefore all mining operations should be suspended when gold is at a premium. During bad times, the task of discovering vacancies is, no doubt, doubly difficult, but it is, for this very reason, doubly necessary. During bad times, there-

[1] W. Dig. pp. 30, 31 ; Min. 5836, 5862-71.

fore—so it may be argued—the labour bureaux should not be set on one side as useless, but rather be supported and strengthened.

And such was the view taken by most of the witnesses that referred to the subject. With a view to facilitating the discovery of vacancies in times of scarcity, it was proposed to affiliate all the labour bureaux in the kingdom under district bureaux controlled by the county and municipal authorities, and to affiliate these district bureaux in their turn under a National Central Labour Bureau conducted by the new Labour Department, which should act as a general " clearing house of labour." All the bureaux—it was contended—should be supported by the rates, and should take no fee from the applicants, whether they be employers or employed. They should not interfere in wage questions, but should leave the parties to make their own bargains and fight their own battles; and they should never accept the registration either of employers wanting men or of men wanting employment, if the want was occasioned by a strike, save and except when such registration was accompanied by a notification of the fact. And, finally, they should never require applicants for registration to produce credentials of character, although they might receive such credentials if voluntarily offered. Mr. John Burns, moreover, in the number of the *Nineteenth Century* before referred to, urged the Government to utilise the 18,000 post offices as employment bureaux, and Mr. Ben Tillett went so far as to suggest that the Poor Law guardians and vestries should have certain statutory powers to compulsorily regulate the influx and outflow of labourers to and from their several districts.

However perfectly the labour bureaux system were organised, it was generally assumed that, at certain seasons, there would not be enough vacancies to go round, and the witnesses, accordingly, addressed themselves to answer the second of the four questions propounded above, *viz.*, how can vacancies be multiplied in existing establishments? The first and most important suggestion made on this point was to reduce the hours of labour by Act of Parliament, but, as this proposal has already been fully discussed in another chapter of the present volume, it may here be dismissed with a passing reference.

·Besides demanding State regulation of the hours of labour, a great many of the witnesses, perceiving that reducing the demand for vacancies was equivalent to increasing the supply, urged the imperative necessity of " doing something" towards the resuscitation of agriculture, with a view to checking the migration of labour from country to town, and so relieving the congestion of the town labour market.

This proposal was put prominently forward by most of the Socialist witnesses, but only one, *viz.*, Mr. W. Ross, representing the National Union of Paper Mill Workers, went so far as to definitely suggest a tax to be placed on imported food.[1] Much of the evidence, indeed, seemed, at first sight, to point in this direction. Thus, Mr. Small, representing the Lanarkshire miners, said: "The country should be more self-sustaining, and more encouragement should

[1] C. III. Dig. p. 80 ; Min. 32647-57, 32661-70.

be given to agriculture, in which direction should be turned much of the labour now given to mining and other mechanical operations. England is not peculiarly well adapted for producing coal,—a commodity which is found in every other country." [1] And Mr. Tom Mann said: "The present condition of agriculture affords a conspicuous object lesson of the failure of sectional control. As foreign nations increase their own production of the goods we sell, our labour and capital should be gradually transferred to the production of the food we buy. At present, too much both of our goods and of our capital goes abroad, when there are plenty of persons at home to be supplied with the former, and employed by the latter. The periodical depressions of English trade are due to the failing credit of the foreign countries for which we cater. The trade we might do at home would not be liable to depression from causes external to ourselves, and it would, therefore, be desirable to be rather more self-supporting." [2]

A closer examination of the evidence, however, will show that, while desiring to induce the agricultural labourer to remain in the country, the Socialist witnesses generally did not intend to convey the idea that they were in favour of the imposition of protective tariffs, in order to make agriculture profitable. Their idea seemed rather to be for the State and county authorities to acquire farms, and, while paying the labourers a sufficient wage to induce them to remain, to keep the prices of corn at the present

[1] A. II. Dig. p. 25 ; Min. 10787-96.
[2] W. Dig. pp. 17, 18.

low figure and make good the deficiency out of the rates and taxes. Thus, Mr Mann said in the passage above quoted that the present condition of agriculture was due to *sectional control*, and, in another passage, that *the State should fulfil its obligation to provide the workless, not only with food*, but also with a fair outlet for their energies.[1]

These statements acquire some point by reading them in connection with the following passage in Mr. Burns' article before referred to, in which he wrote: " In the general interests of the country something must be done to prevent the land lying idle," and, as if to exclude all idea of protection, he added : "*Nothing but the justifiable appropriation by the rural authorities of the uncultivated land will do it.* The creation of parish and district councils must stop this, and, let us hope, will furnish the labourer and farmer with the means not only of cultivation, where now desolation reigns, but will provide the means for more attractive life on the soil, higher wages, and that steadiness of work that will stem the exodus to the towns."

Will provide the means ! But out of what fund ? Obviously, out of the rates ; for, if the industry itself were capable of providing higher wages, etc., a strong believer in Trade Unionism like Mr. Burns would hardly have maintained that " nothing but the appropriation of land by the rural authorities would do it."

Mr. Mann, indeed, would appear to think that, if the public authority were to sink capital in the

1 W. Dig. p. 16.

land, the investment might—even at present prices
—eventually prove profitable, for he said :—" (In
the event of the management of farms by the public
authority), new methods of agriculture would improve
the absolute productivity of British soil, while the
acquisition of small holdings by the labourers might
be expected to improve its productivity relatively to
the soil of other countries."[1] But it is obvious that
the introduction of "new methods of agriculture"
would involve a very large expenditure, which,
for the moment, at any rate, would be unremunera-
tive.

Whether or not there be among the workers an
undercurrent of feeling in favour of protection, the
passages which we have cited from the evidence given
by Messrs. Mann and Small, certainly do seem to be-
tray a tendency to underrate the value of our foreign
trade. How far this is so, the reader can judge for
himself. Perhaps we may, after all, have been in the
habit of rating the value of our foreign trade too
highly. The important point to notice, however, is,
that the Socialists and Trade Unionists certainly
do think we have. This fact was noticed by Sir
Thomas Farrer, who sought to account for it in the
following words :—" There is a desire among Trade
Unions," he said, " to acquire complete control of
production, so as to enable them to dictate the rates
of wages. But the natural effect of such dictation
would be to raise the price of British manufactures,
and cause customers to transfer their custom to foreign

[1] W. Dig. p. 18.

L

markets. The wider, therefore, our foreign trade extends, the more difficult is it for Trade Unions to
make their control of the rates of wages effective.
This is the reason why they are disposed to underrate
the value of our foreign trade, and Mr. Mann himself,
though not desiring to check that trade, yet seems to
regard its possible future extinction with equanimity,
and urges us to produce a larger proportion of our
food instead of fighting to preserve our foreign markets. But,"—so Sir Thomas Farrer argued,—"considering that we are importing two-thirds of our food
from abroad, and that other countries can produce
that food more easily than we can, to suppose that we
can ever become self-supporting is an idle dream.
We should rather determine to repair the loss of old
industries by inventing new ones to supply the new
foreign demands." [1]

To return to the main question before us—how can
vacancies be multiplied?—a third possible solution,
besides State regulation of the hours of labour, and
besides the resuscitation of agriculture, was referred
to by the witnesses, *viz.*, emigration. The few of the
men's representatives, however, that referred to this,
which is, after all, the natural and the historic remedy
for over-population, seemed to regard it, not as a solution of the problem, but rather as equivalent to throwing up the problem in despair. Mr. Mann said it
might do some small good for the moment, but that
no permanently useful result could be expected from
it, inasmuch as it would not have any effect on the
fluctuations of trade, which must always throw men

[1] W. Dig. p. 24 ; Min. 7912-27.

out of work in bad times, so long as they continued to recur. It would be far better, he contended, to check the emigration of capital and develop our unused resources at home than to promote the emigration of labour.[1] On the other hand, Mr. Loch said that he considered emigration to be a satisfactory method as far as it went, although a very careful selection was necessary in order to ensure good results.[2]

Closely connected with the subject of emigration is the proposal made by one or two witnesses to prohibit or restrict the immigration of pauper aliens. Very few witnesses, however, referred to this matter, and some of those who did objected to such prohibition on the ground that the immigrants only competed seriously with British labour in one or two towns, and were for the most part engaged in industries which British workmen liked to support but not to engage in themselves. The evidence of Mr. Giffen on this point is of some interest. He said: "It is a proved fact that the maximum number of foreigners that can possibly have settled in the country in 1891 was 12,000, and it would be dangerous for this country to place restrictions on immigration, for it would furnish our colonies and foreign countries with an excuse, of which they would be only too ready to take advantage, for placing similar restrictions upon the admission into their territories of the emigrants that leave this country in such large numbers."[3]

It was generally admitted—indeed, it is palpably evident—that all these methods of multiplying vacan-

[1] W. Dig. p. 16.   [2] W. App. 97.
[3] W. Dig. p. 43; Min. 7001-10.

cies would, even if effectual, take some time to operate. But the problem of the unemployed is pressing, and will not wait. The witnesses, accordingly, turned their attention to the third question—can work be provided in default of vacancies? The Socialist witnesses were agreed in thinking that it could be provided, and provided to some extent immediately. Sir Thomas Farrer and Mr. Loch, on the other hand, objected to the policy of artificial employment, or employment outside the market demand, as a matter of principle. The last-mentioned witness pointed out that the adoption of such a policy must inevitably have the effect of forcing into pauperism the class immediately above the class it rescued, and that, by merely substituting the labour of the worse class for the labour of the better, it must needs raise the cost of production and intensify the evil it sought to remove.[1] This indictment he proceeded to prove by specific instances, one of which may be quoted. "The Salvation Army," he said, "has established workshops for the employment of the unemployed, and brings the products of their labour into competition, not only with those of the labour of persons that have found work independently, but also with those of the labour of persons for whom work has been provided by other charitable institutions. Thus, the London School Board has accepted the tender of the Salvation Army for supplying firewood to the schools for the next twelve months, in preference to the competing tenders of the Church Army, Dr. Barnardo's Home, and the Boy's Home of Regents' Park."[2] This evidence was

---

[1] W. Dig. pp. 29, 31.   [2] W. Dig. p. 30 ; Min. 5850-2.

not commented on by the Socialist witnesses. But had their attention been called to it, they would probably have replied that artificial employment need not be competitive, if it was managed by State and municipal authorities with the taxes and rates at their back. Those authorities, it would have been said, should take care that the labour of the persons employed on their relief works did not come into competition with the labour of others by utilising it to produce articles, not intended for sale, which, though they might not be actually needed, would be of some public utility.

At all events, the artificial employment advocated by the labour leaders was to be furnished by the public authorities. "Boards of guardians," said Mr. Webb, "should no longer confine themselves to granting charitable relief, but should make some kind of reasonable and honourable provision for exceptional cases of temporary distress, inasmuch as public charity is only one degree less demoralising than private, and should be resorted to only in the very last extremity." [1] Mr. Loch's contention was, of course, the direct opposite. According to him, artificial employment, never being remunerative except at the expense of other labourers, in which case it is a positive evil, is at best only charity in a veiled form, and without the advantages which charity open and avowed possesses. Charity, for example, can adapt its mode of relief to the peculiarities of individual cases, which artificial employment cannot. The charity fund, moreover, evaporates with the wants it supplies, whereas the

[1] W. Dig. p. 21 ; Min. 4392-7.

funds of artificial employment remain, to form a permanent temptation to the recipients to remain idle. A strict administration of the present Poor Law and a rigid application of the workhouse test, supplemented by an equally wise administration of independent systems of charitable relief, seemed to Mr. Loch to be the best policy to pursue.[1]

Artificial employment, however, is no new thing, and the question of its utility or the reverse can best be decided by studying the experiments that have already been made in this direction. Such are Labour Colonies. This method of providing work was mentioned with approval by Mr. Keir Hardie, who intimated that an attempt was being made to obtain a portion of the Scotch Equivalent Grant for the purpose of founding one of these colonies after the model sketched by Mr. H. V. Mills in his book on "Poverty and the State." The persons settled in them, Mr. Keir Hardie contended, should be allowed to send the produce of dairy farms and orchards, but not manufactured goods, to outside markets. The initial cost should be met by doubling the Poor Rate for one year, and the colonies should, in return, be charged with the future maintenance of the poor and aged, in addition to that of the unemployed. Even if the colonies could not pay their way, Mr. Keir Hardie concluded that it would be better to find these persons employment at the cost of the community than to maintain them, still at the cost of the community, in idleness.[2]

---

[1] W. Dig. pp. 29, 30 ; App. 91-96.
[2] A. II. Dig. p. 28 ; Min. 12590, 13144, 13279-87.

But what say the facts? Labour Colonies on sub-
stantially similar lines to those laid down by Mr. Keir
Hardie have been established in Austria, Germany,
Belgium, and, above all, in Holland. Have they succeeded? Mr. Keir Hardie contended that they had.
But Mr. Loch, who furnished a very full account of
their working, maintained that they were all of them
failures, both financially and also because, instead of
raising the efficiency of the colonists and enabling
them to stand alone, they were constantly invaded by
the return of the men that had already passed through
them unreformed.[1] And this conclusion is fully supported by the information contained in the reports on
the Labour Question in Foreign Countries, published
by the Commission.

In his condemnation of Labour Colonies, Mr. Loch
was for once in agreement with Mr. Burns, who stated
in the course of the interesting article from which
we have already quoted :—" Of all the fiscal, charitable
or economic nostrums that are hourly preached for
the redemption of mankind, Labour Colonies are the
least scientific. If municipalisation of agriculture is
intended, that is something I can understand, but that
for years is not likely to prove a remedy for the
workless. Rather will it come after easier things
have been undertaken and accomplished. And should
the municipalisation of agriculture be undertaken on
Socialist lines, its initial stage must be conducted, not
by the unskilled unemployed, plus an in-and-out army
of loafers, casuals, and wastrels (such as Labour
Colonies invariably contain), but by the best of labour

---

[1] W. Dig. pp. 29, 30.

attracted by those better conditions which would accompany such an undertaking started by people with brains, along the lines followed by the London County Council in doing its own work. The argument that the produce of Labour Colonies should be used and consumed inside and should not be sold to people outside is absurd, and presupposes that the colony is sufficiently large to include the numerous trades that are required to supply the wants of a working-class population, and that the organisation should be such as could only be arrived at after years of experiment. The experience of Labour Colonies, moreover, proves that they can only be conducted by earnest, intelligent, unselfish men, or by the most absolute discipline, on a prison labour basis, which the honest unemployed would not tolerate. The fact is, the Labour Colony advocates assume the absence of home ties, associations, and the strong and laudable desire among the genuine unemployed to be so situated in their temporary work in depressed times as would permit of them seizing the first opportunity to leave and return to their proper industries. Men destitute of these qualities lack the essentials for continuous work, and generally would be a source of demoralisation. The Labour Colony, in short, as a remedy for the unemployed is, I maintain, foredoomed to failure, and is nothing but the revival in another form of the hated casual ward with all its physical and moral iniquities."

Mr. Burns, however, was in favour of artificial employment being provided by public authorities in other ways. Thus, he wrote in the same article:—" I believe there are many useful works of general sanitary character that could be carried out by the local authorities in each district, which, combined with repairs of roads, streets, and sewers, would give employment to a total of 24,000 to 30,000 men in London alone, or about 200,000 throughout the country. And why should not this be done ? When a thrifty housewife has an opportunity of an additional cleaning, it is undertaken. Why, then, should not the community utilise its surplus labour that must be kept somehow, and give to its cities and towns, its roads and buildings, that winter and spring cleaning they require ? "

Mr. Loch handed in various documents showing that, in certain specific cases, the policy indicated by Mr. Burns had been rewarded with but doubtful success. On the other hand, Mr. Burns quoted the opinion of an official of the Local Government Board, under whose auspices the policy in question had been partially carried out, to the effect that " the carrying out of relief works possesses certain obvious advantages. The work is possibly done somewhat more cheaply than when labour is in demand."

Satisfactory or the reverse as artificial employment may be, it is clear that expectation and demand for it is increasing among the workers, and that the policy of satisfying such demands is being more and more thoroughly embraced by successive Governments. Thus, Mr. Chamberlain, when President of the Local Government Board, in 1886, addressed a circular to relieving officers, ordering them to send applicants for relief to the relief works provided by the various vestries, *e.g.* at Chelsea and Nottingham, without Poor

Law tests.   And the circular addressed by Mr. Fowler
to the clerks to sanitary authorities on September 30th,
1893, marks a further step in the direction indicated.
It requests the sanitary authorities to forthwith proceed with the execution of works which, in the
interest of their districts, it is desirable should be
carried out at the time when other employment is
difficult to obtain, and to " make arrangements for the
employment in connection with the works of those
who are recommended by the guardians of the poor
as persons, who, owing to their previous condition
and circumstances, it is undesirable should become
subjects of Poor Law relief."

The mention of " previous condition and circumstances " implies a recognition of the weakest point in
our Poor Law system.   With a laudable desire to
render pauperism less attractive than self-support, the
legislature and the Local Government Board have
modelled their regulations on the standard of comfort
of an imagined " pauper class."   But the unemployed — even the penniless unemployed — do not
belong to any one class.   Broadly speaking, every
trade—indeed, every profession—soon becomes supplied with sufficient persons to satisfy its maximum
requirements; and, owing partly to the spread of
education, the higher trades are becoming, if anything,
more overcrowded than the lower, while the professions
are becoming, if anything, more overcrowded than the
trades.   When bad times come, therefore, as large a
number of persons belonging to the higher as to the
lower classes are thrown out of employment.   Yet the
Poor Law tars them all with the same brush, quite

ignoring the fact that what is luxury to a coster-monger is misery to a working engineer, and impossible for a briefless barrister. The principle of making self-support more attractive than pauperism is, no doubt, a sound one ; but its translation into practice should surely be made relative to the different circumstances of the different persons to whom it is applied.

This criticism holds good against the English Poor Law system, not only as an attempted solution of the question, "How can work be provided?" but also to the last question which we have proposed to consider, " How can relief be given in default of work ? " Such relief is given by the Poor Law only to the aged and incapable, or, in other words, to the obviously unemployable, and, in this case also, it is no respecter of persons.

For this reason, it was generally agreed among the witnesses that some better provision should be made for aged paupers. In further support of this contention, it was pointed out that, under the present system, the number of persons that depended upon the rates for support was far too large, since, for some unexplained reason, the members of the industrial classes were far less ready to save money for insurance against old age than against sickness or accident. Thus, the aged poor constituted one-third of the total number of paupers, and their maintenance cost more than one-third of the total £8,500,000 spent under the Poor Law. It was argued, therefore, that, if by any means an adequate old age insurance fund could be created, the ratepayers would be relieved of a very heavy burden, while the old people would, at the same time, be made more comfortable.

With this object in view, Mr. Booth, in his book entitled " Pauperism, a Picture ; and the Endowment of Old Age, an Argument," a work summarised by the secretary to the Commission, and treated as documentary evidence, writes to the following effect: " An examination of other schemes has proved that, to be effectual, any system whereby men are encouraged to contribute during their youth to their support when they are old must be universal, or else the improvident will still trust to the rates. In order to be universal, however, it must be compulsory, and any compulsory method of contribution, universally enforced, is a form of taxation. *It is proposed, therefore, that every man and woman should be entitled to a pension of 5s. per week, at the age of 65, to be paid two-thirds out of the taxes, and one-third out of the rates.* There are at present about 1,323,000 persons over 65 in England and Wales. At 5s. per week each, a universal pension list would reach £17,000,000. Putting, therefore, the total national income at £1,000,000,000 per annum, and assuming that taxation falls, or can be arranged to fall, in true proportion to income, in order to maintain such a pension scheme, everyone would have to pay about 1¾ per cent. of his income."

Mr. Booth was quite ready to admit that, under this scheme, the rich would pay much more in proportion to what they received than would the poor, and that the long-lived would exist on the savings of the short; but he contended that the saving to the ratepayers,

especially in respect of outdoor relief, would be very
great, and that it would simplify the whole problem
of poverty to so large an extent that it was worth
while to consider whether these financial difficulties
could not be overcome.

Mr. Loch opposed all such schemes alike, on the
following grounds. First, that the recognition of the
principle that a large portion of the population has
a right to public maintenance irrespectively of
destitution, is in itself an evil. Secondly, that the
pauperisation of all persons of 65 and upwards would
involve a great economic loss, inasmuch as many
persons of that age are still able to work. Thirdly,
that the direct cost would be enormous, and, finally,
that there is no ground for supposing that thrift
would be encouraged. Poor Law Reform, he urged,
and improved administration are the true line of progress in the matter. Pauperism is an evil to be
prevented rather than cured. The unsatisfactory
physical condition of children is a great cause of
pauperism in later life. Great pains should, therefore,
be bestowed upon the proper physical training of the
young.[1] In his criticism of old age pension schemes,
Mr. Loch was supported by Mr. Giffen, who stated
that a scheme of State insurance, whether against
accidents or for old age pensions, would involve a
very large extension of State officialism and expenditure, in pursuit of an object less useful than many
others towards which they have hitherto been
directed, such as national education, or towards which

[1] W. App. 91-96.

they might be directed, such as the control and endowment of the public hospitals.[1]

With this statement of the case on either side, we will leave the question of old age pensions and the whole problem of the unemployed, of which it forms the concluding part, to the judgment of the reader.

[1] W. Dig. p. 43 ; Min. 7014-28.

PART III.

SPECIAL SUBJECTS.

CHAPTER I.

MINES AND QUARRIES.

Success of the Mines Acts—The Employment of Boys—Deductions for Foreign Substances—The Rights and Duties of Checkweighers—The Qualifications of Colliery Officials—The Timbering of the Working Places—The Right of Miners to examine the Pits—The Employment of "Inexperienced" Persons—Administration of the Coal Mines Regulation Act—Various Proposals—The Metalliferous Mines Regulation Acts.

THE portions of the evidence now about to be summarised relate to the text and administration of certain Acts of Parliament which regulate the conditions of labour in certain special industries. The Acts relating to mines and quarries were, on the whole, pronounced to be a success. Referring to the Coal Mines Regulation Act, 1887, Mr. Jacques, a Northumberland miner, said :—" The legislation we have already got has been of immense benefit to us," [1]

---

[1] A. I. Dig. p. 69 ; Min. 3286.

and Mr. Keir Hardie, of the Ayrshire Miners' Union, said :—" With a few trifling exceptions, the provisions of the Act are quite satisfactory." [1] But their satisfaction with the Act as a whole did not prevent the witnesses desiring a large number of amendments in matters of detail.

The Employment of Boys.—This is a very important question in the mining industry. The actual work of coal getting is dependent upon the performance of several subsidiary operations, and the relative proportion of coal getters, or " hewers " as they are called, and other labourers must always be preserved. Now, " hewing," being highly skilled labour, is by far the best paid of all underground work, and the miners object to being put to other work when their age and capabilities allow them to be promoted. There is, accordingly, an urgent demand for boy labour in order to enable all the men to be employed as hewers immediately upon arriving at manhood. And the supply is not equal to the demand.

This scarcity of boys is specially marked in the Durham and Northumberland coal-fields, but it would seem to be felt to some extent also in South Wales, where two of the witnesses, representing the employers' interest, admitted that circumstances sometimes compelled the law regulating the hours of boy labour to be broken, thus giving rise to not infrequent prosecutions. The best proof of this scarcity, however, is furnished by the fact that the hours of

[1] A. II. Dig. p. 28 ; Min. 12921.

the boys are often longer than those of the men. In Durham and Northumberland, indeed, the boys ordinarily work the full legal limit of ten, whereas the "hewers" work only seven and a half hours a day. For this state of affairs the law is itself partly responsible. Section 4 of the Coal Mines Regulation Act has artificially intensified the scarcity complained of by prohibiting the employment underground of any boy under twelve. The provision is, no doubt, a wise one; but it certainly has the effect of increasing the pressure brought upon those that remain eligible for employment.

In addition to this, the want of uniformity in the provisions of the Mines and the Factory Acts tends still further to reduce the number of boys available for mining. For factories are allowed to take them at the age of eleven, and, as was pointed out by Mr. Macalpine, the representative of the South Lancashire and Cheshire Coal Owners' Association, the result is that the factories obtain most of the boys that would otherwise be available for the mines a year later.[1] It was, therefore, proposed to lower the age at which boys may begin to work underground in mines to eleven, and, at the same time, to extend their legal period of employment to 60 hours a week.

Most of the Durham and Northumberland miners' representatives were not in favour of either of these proposals, but were less opposed to the second than to the first. They seemed to regard the scarcity of boys as a guarantee that their own hours would not be increased, and they would rather the boys employed in

[1] A. I. Dig. p. 31 ; Min. 6190-203, 6259, 6400-17.

M

mines were few and hard worked, than that they should either be sufficiently numerous to enable the " hewers " to work longer, or be worked sufficiently lightly to prevent them from being promoted to the ranks of the hewers as soon as they were grown up. As Mr. R. Young pointed out, a shortening of the miners' hours during boyhood, would cause many additional men to be employed at the supplementary work which boys have to do, and so would prevent the same boys from working, as hewers, at still shorter hours during their early manhood. In fact, a reduction of the hours of persons under sixteen would involve a corresponding increase in the hours of persons between sixteen and twenty.[1]

The miners in the other districts did not share the objections of their brethren in Durham and Northumberland to reducing the hours of boy labour. On the contrary, they desired the hours for both boys and adults to be limited by law to eight per day. And, if the supply of boys proved insufficient to admit of the present output being maintained under the proposed arrangement, they would be only too pleased to see production checked, and prices raised in proportion. In fact, the difference of opinion between the miners in the north of England and in other districts in this matter results from the difference in general policy explained above in the chapter on Hours of Labour. On one point, however, the miners of all districts were agreed—that, in spite of the demand for boy labour, the legislature ought

[1] A. I. Dig. p. 16 ; Min. 2159, 2164, 2235, 2326, 2386.

not only not to lower the standard of age to eleven,
but to raise it to thirteen.

Deductions for Foreign Substances.—Section 12 of
the Coal Mines Regulation Act provides that all piece-
workers, *i.e.*, all hewers, shall be paid " according to
the actual weight gotten by them of the mineral con-
tracted to be gotten." That the mineral gotten by
them " shall be truly weighed at a place as near to
the pit mouth as is reasonably practicable." And
that employers and employed may enter into an
agreement concerning deductions in respect of foreign
substances mixed with the coal. In accordance
with this section, such agreements have been made
in every mining district. In most cases, the amount
of the deductions is determined by weighing the
foreign substances in respect of which they are
made, but, in some, as for example in Lanarkshire, a
certain deduction seems to be made on every tub of
coal indiscriminately. The adoption of both these
methods of assessment at once, as was alleged to be
sometimes the case, was characterised by Mr. Smellie,
representing the Lanarkshire miners, as most unjust.[1]
The same witness also complained of the custom of
treating agreements as to deductions as implied in the
contract of service, and desired the legislature to insert
in the Act a clause to the effect that no such agreement should be deemed to exist unless made expressly
and in definite terms.[2] In all districts, moreover, the
subject seemed to give rise to a great deal of friction,

[1] A. II. Dig. p. 24 ; Min. 9811.
[2] A. II. Dig. p. 24 ; Min. 9870-1.

and Mr. T. Richards of the South Wales and Monmouthshire Miners' Federation went so far as to
suggest that, for this reason, the permission extended
to employers and employed to enter into agreements
respecting deductions for foreign substances should
be withdrawn.[1]   On the other hand, it was pointed
out by Mr. Edward Jones, representing the Coal
Owners' Association in the same district, that the
present provisions of the law were very necessary,—
indeed, that they wanted strengthening, because the
practice of sending out dust and refuse mixed with
the coal even now involved a cost to the employers
of nearly 6d. a ton.[2]   Mr. A. K. M'Cosh, representing
the Lanarkshire Coal Masters' Association, moreover,
defended the deductions on the ground that, though
the majority of the workmen could be depended on
to put out " clean " coal, a considerable minority could
not, and added that it was to the employers' interest
to adjust their scales of deductions in such a way as
not to bear hardly upon the former, while being at
the same time sufficiently exacting to prevent the
latter from filling rubbish.[3]

Indeed, the deductions in question were generally
admitted to be quite justifiable in spite of the frequent
quarrels that they occasioned.   Messrs. Patterson and
Wilson, representing the Durham Miners' Association,
pointed out that the grievances connected with them,
after all, only affected individuals.   To the miners as
a class, they were rather the source of advantage,

-[1] A. I. Dig. p. 70 ; Min. 5832.
[2] A. II. Dig. p. 18 ; Min. 11685.
[3] A. II. Dig. p. 31 ; Min. 13627-91, 13698-704.

because the better the quality of the coals sent to the market, the higher the prices, and the higher, therefore, the wages.[1] And, in the majority of cases, the scale of the deductions does not appear to be excessive. Thus, Mr. Keir Hardie said that, in some collieries, the amount deducted scarcely covered the cost of separating the coal from the refuse.[2]

The Rights and Duties of Checkweighers.—A checkweigher is, as the name implies, a person appointed by the miners to check the weighing by which the deductions for foreign substances are determined. The Act compels the employers to allow such appointments to be made, and to afford the appointee "every facility for enabling him to fulfil his duties," while, on the other hand, it provides that the checkweigher "shall not be authorised in any way to impede or interrupt the working of the mine, or to interfere with the weighing, or with any of the workmen, or with the management of the mine ; but shall be authorised only to . . . take a correct account of the weight of the mineral, or to determine correctly the deductions, as the case may be." It is further provided that "it shall be lawful for the owner or manager of any mine, by agreement with the workmen, to retain the agreed contribution out of the wages of the workmen for the payment of the checkweigher . . . and to pay and account for the same to the checkweigher."

These provisions leave many loop-holes for evasion.

[1] A. I. Dig. p. 8 ; Min. 449.
[2] A. II. Dig. p. 29 ; Min. 12682-9.

Thus, although employers are compelled to allow the men to appoint a checkweigher, there is apparently nothing to prevent them dismissing all their hands and offering to re-engage them on condition that any given appointment which they may have made be cancelled. Mr. Smellie, representing the Lanarkshire miners, stated that this mode of evasion had been declared legal by the Scotch Court of Session, and quoted two cases in which it had been resorted to.[1] The impeachment was admitted by Mr. M'Cosh, the representative of the coal owners in the same district; but he explained that the men's checkweighers were objected to only when and because they interfered with the colliers by assisting the Union pickets to prevent free labourers going to work, etc. "Check-weighers," he added, "certainly fulfil useful functions, but offences of this kind are sufficiently common among them to make it preferable to let the weighing be done by neutral officials, and so render check-weighing unnecessary."[2]

It was the opinion of Mr. J. B. Atkinson, Her Majesty's Inspector of Mines for the East Scotland district, however, that the men had a genuine griev-ance in regard to the evasions of the law which Mr. M'Cosh sought to justify. Anything that tended to impair the men's absolute freedom in the choice of their checkweigher was, he contended, a violation of the spirit of the Act."[3]

Again, the sections of the Act quoted above invite

[1] A. II. Dig. p. 24 ; Min. 9979-82, 10088-98.
[2] A. II. Dig. p. 31 ; Min. 13630-3, 13705-15.
[3] A. II. Dig. p. 33 ; Min. 18663-7.

evasion by the indefinite nature of the terms they contain. For example, employers are required to afford the men's checkweighers "every facility" for performing their duties. It was the opinion of Mr. Smellie that "every facility" was not afforded unless the checkweighers were accommodated with some better shelter than that of the pit head.[1] The employers held otherwise, and Mr. Atkinson, the inspector for East Scotland, agreed with them so far as to think that the Act gave him no power to enforce compliance with what he considered to be a reasonable demand.[2]

The owners themselves, moreover, have a grievance in the vague wording of the section of the Act which prohibits checkweighers from impeding or interrupting the working of the mine. Mr. M'Cosh complained that it was in consequence of this vagueness that checkweighers were able with impunity to act as permanent Union pickets, and he considered that they should, at all events, be definitely forbidden to give a third party information about a man's time or output without that man's consent.[3]

In spite of these loopholes for evasion, the provisions of the Act relating to the rights and duties of checkweighers seem to be generally respected. It was only in the Scotch mining districts, where organisation is comparatively weak, that the matter seemed to cause any friction at all, and, even in Scotland, both parties were at heart agreed as to the advantages

[1] A. II. ; Min. 10056.
[2] A. II. Dig. p. 33 ; Min. 18676-7.
[3] A. II. Dig. p. 31 ; Min. 13630-3, 13705-15.

of the present system. Mr. M'Cosh himself stated that, though checkweighers sometimes exceeded their functions, they were, as a rule, the means of saving much trouble and irritation on the score of weighing, and that employers entertained no general objection to their appointment.[1] The practical advantages of the system of paying the checkweighers by allowing the employers to deduct the requisite sum from the wages of the miners, were so fully recognised by the Ayrshire colliers that they desired it to be made compulsory, instead of merely lawful.[2]

The Qualifications of Colliery Officials.—Sections 20, 21 and 23 of the Act include the following provisions :—

Section 20. " A person shall not be qualified to be a manager of a mine, unless he is for the time being registered as the holder of a first-class certificate under this Act."

Section 21. " Every person so nominated (*i.e.*, every under manager), must hold either a first-class or second class certificate under this Act."

Section 23. " There shall be two descriptions of certificates of competency under this Act—(i.) first-class certificates, that is to say, certificates of fitness to be manager, and (ii.) second-class certificates, that is to say, certificates of fitness to be under manager; but no person shall be entitled to a certificate under this Act unless he shall have had practical experience in a mine for at least five years. For the purpose of grant-

[1] A. II. Dig. p. 31 ; Min. 13630-32, 13705-15.
[2] A. II, Dig. p. 28 ; Min. 12564,

ing, in any part of the United Kingdom to be from
time to time defined by an order from the Secretary
of State, certificates of competency for the purposes
of this Act, examiners shall be appointed, etc."

The wisdom of these provisions was generally admitted, inasmuch as it is upon the ability of managers
and under managers that the safe working of the
mines so largely depends. The only amendment proposed was to introduce analogous tests in the case of
foremen and roadsmen, some of whom were alleged by
Mr. Small, representing the Lanarkshire miners, to be
grossly incompetent.[1]

The Timbering of the Working Places.—The task
of setting pieces of timber to support the roof and
keep up the sides after the coal has been cut away by
the hewers, is partly performed by a special class of
workers ; but, as there is a strict limit to the number
of persons that can be employed in the narrow working places without getting into one another's way, the
hewers have to do a large portion of it themselves ;
and, since they are paid according to the weight of
coal they get, they are tempted to neglect this important subsidiary operation, and many accidents occur
in consequence. Recognising the importance of giving the miners no excuse for this dangerous neglect
of duty, the legislature has inserted in the Act the
following provision :—

" Where the timbering of the working places is
done by the workmen employed therein, suitable
timber shall be provided at the working place, gate-

[1] A. II. Dig. p. 24 ; Min. 10175.

end, pass-bye, siding or other similar place in the
mine convenient to the workmen, and the distance
between the sprags or holing props, where they are
required, shall not exceed six feet or such less distance
as may be ordered by the owner, agent or manager."

It was the opinion of Messrs. Smellie[1] and Keir
Hardie[2] that the law was not stringent enough on
this point, and the latter proposed to amend it by
omitting the words " gate-end, pass-bye, siding or
other similar place in the mine convenient to the
workmen," thus causing the prop wood to be always
placed actually in the working places.   Mr. Atkinson,
the inspector for East Scotland, moreover, stated that
he sometimes found that the carriage of timber from
the pit to the face was not properly organised, and
added that the matter was of very great importance,
because 50 per cent. of the many accidents that occurred in mines were attributable to the falling in of
roofs and sides.[3]   On the other hand, it was the
opinion of Mr. M'Cosh that to demand a stack of
various sizes of timber to be placed in every working
place was most unreasonable,[4] and Mr. Jacob Ray, a
South Wales mine manager, stated that there was
such a thing as timbering too much, and that he had
known cases where a good roof had been converted
into a bad one by the excessive use of prop wood.[5]

[1] A. II. ; Min. 10009.
[2] A. II. Dig. p. 28 ; Min. 12564, 12909-20.
[3] A. II. Dig. p. 33; Min. 18659-60, 18667-70, 18739-45,
18792-6.
[4] A. II. Dig. p. 32 ; Min. 13655-6.
    A. II. Dig. p. 16 ; Min. 11088-95.

The prevalence of accidents from falling roofs and sides appeared to be specially marked in the South Wales district, where the roof is peculiarly brittle and dangerous. As Mr. Davies, the manager of the Cwmaman Collieries, pointed out:—" No Acts of Parliament, no inspectors, and no scientific appliances can wholly eliminate from the mines the natural sources of danger, or remove the necessity for constant care on the part of every man engaged in so dangerous an industry. The chief aim of the legislature should, therefore, be to continue to teach the miners the importance of taking care of their own lives and limbs." [1]

The Right of Miners to Examine the Pits.—Partly with the object of encouraging carefulness among the miners, a further provision has been made to the effect that " the persons employed in a mine may appoint two of their number, or any two persons, not being mining engineers, who are practical working miners, to inspect the mine at their own cost," and that " every facility shall be afforded by the owner, agent, and manager, and all persons in the mine, for the purpose of the inspection." The workmen, however, only avail themselves of this right in 10 per cent. of the mines in the kingdom, and, in these few cases, the employers generally pay a portion of the cost. Some of the men's representatives attributed failure to appoint inspectors to fear of being "victimised," but the evidence did not show any ground for such fear. On the contrary, the employers' representatives unanimously expressed regret that the men did not avail themselves of their right of

[1] A. II. Dig. p. 18 ; Min. 11459, 11605-15.

inspection more often, and Mr. Atkinson said he would be glad to see the work of the Government inspectors better supplemented by the action of the men themselves.[1] In fact, the only real obstacle in the way of the men exercising their right of inspection appears to be the expense. Mr. J. M. Ronaldson, Her Majesty's Inspector of Mines for the West Scotland district, informed the Commission that, when he had asked Mr. Keir Hardie to persuade the men to appoint inspectors, the answer he received was that the men "had no intention of undertaking duties for the performance of which he (Mr. Ronaldson) was well paid."[2] Apart from the expense, however, the men's representatives declared that the right of inspection was appreciated, and would be acted on, if checkweighers and miners' agents, who would be able to examine the pits without special payment, were made eligible for appointment. It was, therefore, proposed to insert the words "or have been" between the words "who are," and the words "practical working miners" in the above quoted section of the Act. On the other hand, it was pointed out by Mr. W. Thomas, of the Monmouthshire and South Wales Owners' Association, that it would be worse than useless to entrust the task of examining and criticising the condition of a pit to persons, like checkweighers, who had lost touch with its working, or, like miners' agents, who, perhaps, had never possessed any acquaintance with it at all.

[1] A. II. Dig. p. 32 ; Min. 18652-3, 18712-28, 18749-50, 18763-7.

[2] A. II. Dig. p. 34 ; Min. 18846-7.

It is only the miners' intimate knowledge of the pits that makes their inspections valuable.[1]

The Employment of "Inexperienced" Persons.—The Act of 1887 contains the following new and important provision:—" No person . . . . shall be allowed to work alone as a coal or ironstone getter in the face of the workings, until he has had two years' experience of such work under the supervision of skilled work-men, or unless he shall have been previously employed for two years in or about the face of the workings of a mine." If this provision were perfectly enforced, the effect would virtually be to introduce a system of compulsory apprenticeship, and thus to give consider-able assistance to the miners' Unions in their efforts to control admissions to the industry. Up to the present, however, its operation has been impeded by two facts. First, that, by an error in draughtsmanship, the section has been capable of being interpreted to mean that, though inexperienced men may not work in solitude, two or more of them may work in company without the co-operation of skilled miners; and secondly, that, owing to the migratory habits of colliers as a class, it is impossible to determine whether candidates for employment really possess the necessary experience which they invariably claim.

The first point was the subject of a great number of complaints on the part of the men's representatives, but it did not appear to have been taken advantage of by the employers, if for no other reason, because no

[1] A. II. Dig. p. 20 ; Min. 11900-8, 11947-55, 12005-20, 12049-71.

court of law had been given an opportunity of actually making the interpretation complained of. The defect in draughtsmanship seems to have impeded the operation of the law through the inspectors' fear of what might be, rather than through their knowledge of what would be, the result of taking a case into court. It is the second point—the difficulty of testing a newcomer's claim to the necessary experience —that constitutes the real impediment to the operation of the law. In times of increasing trade, it is impossible to forbid an employer to take, from among the crowd of strangers that throng the neighbourhood of his pits at such seasons, any of the additional hands which the exigencies of his trade so imperatively demand, simply on the ground that he can test the alleged claims of none of them. The legislature has recognised this by expressly exempting employers from responsibility for the misrepresentations of workmen on this point. It was the opinion of the miners' representatives, however, that the difficulty might be overcome by requiring miners, after serving the statutory two years' apprenticeship, to obtain a certificate of competency from a joint examining board of employers and employed. Then, they urged, it would be possible to forbid employers to engage men who could not produce their certificates. Mr. E. Jones, representing the South Wales colliery owners, made a counter proposal to the effect that managers should be required to give all men leaving their service signed documents showing the duration and conditions of their former employment, and, conversely, to demand such documents from all applicants for skilled

employment.[1] This proposal, however, did not find
favour with the miners, for its adoption would involve
a surrender of the control of admissions to the trade
which they want to acquire.

Several other proposals were made proving
the contentious nature of the subject. Thus, the
men desired the period of apprenticeship or probation
to be extended to five years, whereas the employers
wished to reduce it to eighteen months, and to
specialise the experience of six of the eighteen.
Again, the men's representatives proposed to make
managers liable to prosecution, without the consent
of the inspector or Secretary of State being obtained,
in respect of the acts done by the inexperienced men
they might employ, and to compel employers to pay
"skilled" men at higher wages than the "unskilled"
men with whom they were associated; both of which
proposals were naturally distasteful to the employers.
In fact, the amendment of the law relating to the
employment of "inexperienced" persons seems to
have furnished each party with a means of furthering
its own interest in respect of the point at which it is
brought into antagonism with the other. The employers want to become independent of the Unions,
and the Unions want to make themselves necessary to
the employers. Both, therefore, want to control the
admissions to the trade, and the legislature, which has
already acknowledged the necessity of regulating
those admissions in some way, has to decide between
them. The 39th general rule under the 49th section
of the Act of 1887, inclines to the side of the Unions;

[1] A. II. Dig. p. 19 ; Min. 11684, 11722-4, 11793-4, 11809-12.

but, until it is further amended in one way or the other, it will continue inoperative to the detriment of the paramount interests of safety which it was intended to serve.

Administration.—Mr. David Morgan, representing the Aberdare and Merthyr Miners' Association, said : " The inspection of the mines is inadequate and inefficient," [1] and Mr. Smellie, representing the Lanarkshire miners, went so far as to remark that the majority of the miners had not the slightest faith in the present system of Government inspection,[2] while Mr. Weeks, representing the Northumberland Coal Owners' Association, said that the appointment of Government inspectors had not increased the safety of the mines.[3]

In spite of these strictures, however, the inspectors were not accused of positive neglect of duty or incompetency by any of the witnesses with the single exception of Mr. Keir Hardie,[4] and the value of his criticism is somewhat discounted by the evidence relating to his personal relations with the inspector for the West of Scotland district against whom they were directed.[5]

The complaints of the witnesses on this point may have been partly due to a misapprehension of what the inspectors' duties really are. As was pointed out

[1] A. I. Dig. p. 23 ; Min. 4233-7.
[2] A. II. Dig. p. 25 ; Min. 10026.
[3] A. I. Dig. p. 76 ; Min. 3252.
[4] A. II. Dig. p. 27; Min. 12521-40.
[5] A. II. Dig. pp. 33, 34, 35.

by several of the colliery managers that gave evidence before the Commission, as well as by the inspectors themselves, to trust mainly to Government inspection for the safety of the mines is certain to result in disappointment. Even if the staff were largely increased, the inspectors could not visit the pits sufficiently often to guarantee freedom from the danger which becomes apparent in different places every day and almost every hour. The only duty that they can hope to discharge efficiently is to see that inspection is properly performed by the colliery authorities, on whom the responsibility for the proper observance of the Act is placed. Their primary function, in short, is not to inspect the mines, but to inspect the inspection of mines.

It is, however, impossible to imagine that so determined an attack upon the administration should be wholly based upon a misapprehension of what seems to be so obvious a fact. For the real motive of the attack we must look elsewhere, and on a closer examination of the evidence it will be found that the blows inflicted by the various parties interested in the trade upon the inspectors were, in reality, directed against one another.

Whatever be the necessary limitations of a Government inspector's functions, it is clear that he is a very important personage. To him belongs the power of setting the law in motion, and with him, consequently, the decision of disputes arising out of the interpretation of the Act primarily rests. Broadly speaking, therefore, the inspectors are constantly being urged by the men to do too much, and by the employers to

N

do too little, and whatever course they pursue they are certain to dissatisfy either one party or both.

Among the most obvious of the devices open to each party in order to get the ear of the inspector is to secure the selection of a member of its own class for the post. At present, the inspectors are generally chosen from among colliery managers, who are, on the whole, in sympathy with the owners. The men, accordingly, desire to obtain the appointment for "practical working miners," and, inasmuch as the qualifying examination is too high for them to pass, they proposed that the standard should be lowered to suit them. To this proposal the owners and colliery managers advanced the very pertinent objection that it would never do to appoint to inspectorships persons possessed of lower qualifications than the managers whose actions they were to supervise and criticise— indeed, the colliery managers took the opportunity of proposing that, in addition to the possession of first-class certificates which is at present required, five years' experience of management should be demanded of all candidates for the post. In many cases, the men seemed to appreciate the force of this objection, but they contended that it would cease to apply if working men were appointed, not to supersede, but to assist the existing inspectors. And it was the desire to justify this proposed increase in the staff that furnished the real motive for proving Government inspection to be at present inadequate.

It is unfortunate that, in regard to this matter, no really disinterested evidence could be obtained. Even the present inspectors, to whom one would generally look for an impartial opinion, could hardly be expected to assist the men in proving the inefficiency of the body to which they belonged, especially when they could not but feel that it was the ultimate aim of their critics to supersede them. The only verdict that can be given is that the burden of proof in this matter undoubtedly rested with the men, and that they did not make out nearly so strong a case for the appointment of additional working men inspectors in the case of mines as was done in the case of factories. The Government would hardly be justified in sanctioning additional expenditure in salaries for inspectors of mines merely on the strength of the evidence given before the Commission.

Other proposals made by the witnesses connected with the mining industry were: To make the mining department independent of the Home Office, to insert a clause in the Coal Mines Regulation Act forbidding the double shift system, to make foremen officially subordinate to the Government inspectors, to prohibit employers from selling coal at a lower price than would enable them to pay a certain fixed minimum wage, to fix a maximum rate of profits, and to limit the hours of coal drawing to eight per day.

The Metalliferous Mines Regulation Act of 1872.— This Act applies to underground quarries, *i.e.*, to mines other than those of coal, stratified ironstone, shale and fire-clay, which are under the Coal Mines Regulation Act. The representatives of the North Wales Quarrymen's Union wanted to extend its application to open quarries, and the quarry owners themselves considered that both open and closed quarries should be subjected to uniform treatment, but they thought such uniformity ought to be attained by abolishing Government regulation in the case of closed quarries, rather than by introducing it in the case of open ones. The men also complained of the administration of the Metalliferous Mines and the Coal Mines Regulation Acts being entrusted to the same staff. The present inspectors, they contended, might understand coal mines, but they knew nothing at all about quarries, which ought to be looked after by a special staff of "practical men." They also complained because the inspectors had ceased to incorporate in their official reports statistics relating to quarries, and they considered that every quarry proprietor should be obliged to send to the Home Office annual returns respecting the total make in tons and value, the number of men employed, the wages paid, and the working expenses.

CHAPTER II.

The Merchant Shipping Acts—Local Marine Boards—Engagement of Seamen—Allotment of Wages—Provisions—Cases of Illness—Accommodation on board Ship—Unseaworthiness of Ships—Desertion—Deck Cargoes—Rating of Seamen—Watertight Compartments—Presence of Unauthorised Persons on board Ship—The Canal Boats Acts—The Metropolitan Public Carriages Act—The Railway Regulation Acts.

The Merchant Shipping Acts, 1854-1890.—"There is no trade in the world," said Mr. J. Cormack, representing the Shipping Federation, "which has been so harassed with legislation as the shipping trade. We have had Acts at the rate of three and four in a year, so that we scarcely know where we are."[1] The enormous bulk of the Bill, filling some 350 pages, which Mr. Mundella has introduced into the House of Commons, to consolidate the various Acts relating to merchant shipping, seems to prove this statement to be hardly exaggerated.

The subject may most conveniently be treated under the following heads : (1) Local Marine Boards, (2) Engagement of Seamen, (3) Allotment of Wages, (4) Provisions, (5) Cases of Illness, (6) Accommodation

[1] B. II. Dig. p. 119.

on board Ship, (7) Unseaworthiness of Ships, (8)
Desertion, (9) Deck Cargoes, Overloading, etc., (10)
Rating of Seamen, Discharges, etc., (11) Watertight
Compartments, and (12) Presence of Unauthorised
Persons on board Ship.

Local Marine Boards are constituted subject to the
provisions of sections 110-121, and section 241 of the
Merchant Shipping Act of 1854. They are composed
of local magistrates, representatives of the shipowners,
and nominees of the Board of Trade. The last
mentioned, however, are generally shipowners also,
and Mr. J. Havelock Wilson, representing the
National Amalgamated Seamen's and Firemen's Union,
proposed to compel the Board of Trade always to
nominate independent persons.[1] Sir Henry Calcraft,
on the other hand, representing the said Board, intimated that its policy was always to nominate suitable
persons belonging to, or in sympathy with, the seaman
class, where such could be found. Mr. Wilson
further suggested that the Seamen's Union at every
port should directly elect six additional persons to sit
on the Local Marine Board. Although, as was pointed
out by Mr. Scrutton[2] and Sir Henry Calcraft,[3] the
judicial functions of the boards extend only to alleged
misconduct on the part of certificated officers, Messrs.
Wilson and Plimsoll[4] claimed that seamen were, nevertheless, immediately interested in those functions
being properly discharged, and the last named witness

[1] B. I. Dig. p. 63 ; Min. 9348-51.
[2] B. II. Dig. p. 103 ; Min. 14087.
[3] B. II. Dig. p. 103 ; Min. 14805-7.
[4] B. II. Dig. p. 103 ; Min. 11310-2.

considered that they should be enabled to secure the transfer of such cases as did concern their interests from the jurisdiction of the Local Marine Board to that of the nearest magistrate who was not a ship-owner.

Engagements of seamen[1] are regulated by sections 146-167 of the same Act of 1854. According to the provisions of section 147, no person other than, the owner, master or mate, or some person who is *bonâ fide* the servant and in the constant employ of the owner or master, may engage or supply any sea-man to any ship in the United Kingdom without a special license from the Board of Trade. Inasmuch as the said Board has refused to grant such a license to the agents of the Shipping Federation, Messrs. Laws and Morrison, as representatives of that body, pro-posed to amend the law, so as to entitle them to supply men without applying to the Board of Trade at all, by substituting the word "agent" for the word "servant," and omitting the words "in the constant employ." As matters stand at present, the Shipping Federation and other corporations and individuals were alleged to be constantly breaking the law by illegally supplying men to ships, and this was admitted to be the case by Mr. Laws himself. Sir Henry Calcraft, while claiming that the Board of Trade had materially diminished the practice of " crimping " as offences against this law are called, considered that no further enactment would suffice to entirely stamp it out.

Allotment of wages[2] is dealt with in sections 149-169

[1] B. I. Dig. pp. 63, 64 ; B. II. Dig. pp. 103, 104, 108.
[2] B. I. Dig. pp. 64, 65 ; B. II. Dig. p. 106.

of the Act of 1854, and in section 3 of the Merchant
Seamen (Payment of Wages and Rating) Act, 1880.
Messrs. J. Havelock Wilson, J. B. Lee, and W. Key,
representing various seamen's Unions, desired to extend the power of allotment from one-half to two-
thirds of the seaman's wages. The same witnesses
also contended that payments under allotment notes
should begin at the end of a week, Mr. Key
observing that the best thing to be done would be
to abolish allotment notes altogether, and substitute
for them weekly payments to the man's family direct,
beginning from the very first week of his engagement.
It was also pointed out that, under the present
system, the men were in the habit of getting trades-
men, Jews, and other persons to cash their allotment
notes, who, in return for the favour, took the first
month's payment for themselves, thereby obliging
the man's family, in whose favour the notes were
drawn, to wait two months instead of one for
the money. On the other hand, Mr. Smith
Park, representing the Glasgow Shipowners' Association, contended that the more frequent payment
of larger portions of a seaman's wages to his
family by means of allotment notes would weaken
the power of the master to prevent desertions, besides
exposing the seaman himself to the annoyance of
finding, on his return from a long voyage, that his
wages had all been spent.

Provisions[1] must be supplied to seamen in the
manner laid down in sections 149, 221-227 and
232 of the Act of 1854, in section 31 of the

[1] B. I. Dig. pp. 65, 66 ; B. II. Dig. 106-110.

Passengers Act of 1855, and in section 7 of the
Merchant Shipping Act of 1867. The law provides that every agreement shall contain   tement
of the scale of the provisions to be gi   to each
seaman, and that such scale shall be sub   to the
general approval of the Board of Trade. The said
Board has, accordingly, drawn up a minimum scale,
which Messrs. J. Havelock Wilson, J. B. Lee, and
Captain E. B. Hatfield, representing various branches
of the Merchant Service, agreed in thinking insufficient, and the two first named witnesses went so far
as to propose the insertion of a revised scale in the
text of an Act of Parliament. It was pointed out,
however, by the representatives of the employers that
the Board of Trade scale was regarded as a minimum
but not as a standard, and that the provisions actually
supplied were in most cases superior both in quantity,
quality, and variety, to those authorised in the scale.
Indeed, the bill of fare sanctioned by the Board of
Trade was rigidly adhered to only when necessitated
by the exigencies of long voyages, and by way of
punishment for insubordination, etc. Mr. Lee admitted the truth of these statements in some cases,
but denied that they held good universally, and
added that he considered penal reductions of the
men's allowance of provisions to be "a very bad plan."
Sir Henry Calcraft, on the other hand, was of opinion
that the law, as it now stood, afforded quite sufficient
protection to the seamen in the matter of their food
supply. He intimated, however, that the Board of
Trade was instituting inquiries as to how far an improvement could be effected in the matter.

Both Mr. Wilson and Mr. Plimsoll urged the desirability of extending the Act, providing for the inspection of the provisions taken on board of "passenger" ships, to ocean-going vessels that did not carry passengers, and the former witness further complained that Local Marine Boards did not avail themselves of their statutory power of appointing inspectors of stores. Mr. Plimsoll detailed at some length the sufferings inflicted upon sailors in being obliged to consume food of inferior quality, and referred the Commission to a Blue Book on the Health of Crews, dated August 1876. The representatives of the employers, on the other hand, agreed in declaring that the supply of inferior provisions was quite exceptional, and Mr. Raeburn, who represented the Clyde District Committee of the Shipping Federation, maintained that the real ground for complaint, where any such ground existed at all, was not the bad quality of the food itself, but the spoiling of good food by bad cooking, and urged the advisability of adopting better and more systematic methods of procuring competent cooks for the sea service. Mr. J. Scrutton, representing the Chamber of Shipping of the United Kingdom, denied the truth of the allegations made by Mr. Plimsoll, who, he pointed out, had himself qualified them by the remark—"I should mislead your lordship (the Earl of Derby) if I wanted you to suppose that that is in existence now." Personally, the witness entertained no objection to the inspection of provisions as a matter of principle; but, as a matter of practice, he contended that there were several obstacles to its more general adoption.

Cases of illness [1] are to be provided for in accordance with sections 224-232 of the Act of 1854 and
section 7 of the Act of 1867. Mr. Manton, who represented the National Federation of Fishermen, complained that the Grimsby employers charged the
fishermen for the use of the medicine chests placed on
board the boats belonging to the North Sea fishing
fleet, and Mr. J. Havelock Wilson made three distinct
proposals for the amendment of the law on the point.
First, that, in all cases, shipowners should be required
to retain the services of a qualified medical man at
their own expense; secondly, that, the seamen's
hospital expenses incurred abroad should be paid by
the shipowner, without deduction from the wages;
and, thirdly, that the wages of invalided seamen should
recommence at the moment they left the hospital
and embarked upon their homeward voyage, and should
continue until the moment of their arrival in the
United Kingdom. As the law stands at present, shipowners are liable for such medical expenses only as
are incidental to the employment, and any addition to
their liability in this respect was strongly opposed by
their representatives.

Accommodation on board ship [2] is regulated by
section 9 of the Act of 1867, which provides, among
other things, that " every place in any ship, occupied
by seamen or apprentices and appropriated to their
use, shall have for every such seaman or apprentice a
space of not less than 72 cubic feet, measured on the
deck or floor of such place." The minimum accom-

[1] B. I. Dig. pp. 66, 67 ; B. II. Dig. pp. 110, 111.
[2] B. I. Dig. p. 67 ; B. II. Dig. pp. 111, 112.

modation here ordered to be observed, was characterised by several witnesses as insufficient, and Mr. Wilson proposed to extend it to 120 cubic feet and to compel shipowners to provide a special cabin for the men to use for drying their clothes. It was pointed out, indeed, by Sir Henry Calcraft that the legal minimum of 72 cubic feet per man was quite sufficient, provided that the other legal requirements as to the sanitary and other internal arrangements were fulfilled. That these requirements were not fulfilled, however, was the unanimous testimony of the representatives of the seamen, although one of them, Mr. P. B. Sutcliffe, stated that this was partly due to the slovenly habits of the seamen themselves. In spite of the provisions of the Act, paint, liquors and oil stores were said to be habitually placed in the men's sleeping places, where the ventilation was defective, the protection against wind and weather inadequate, and the general sanitary arrangements positively unwholesome. The representatives of the employers, on the other hand, contended that, in all these respects, there was a marked and steadily increasing improvement throughout the merchant service, and that, as applied to vessels belonging to first-class firms, the charges of bad accommodation preferred by the men's representatives were quite unfounded.

Unseaworthiness of ships[1] is provided against by section 5 of the Act of 1876, which prevents shipowners and masters from contracting out of their obligation to use every reasonable means to secure the fitness of their vessels for sea. Mr. J. Havelock

[1] B. I. Dig. pp. 61, 67, 68 ; B. II. Dig. pp. 113, 114.

Wilson and Captain Hatfield, an officer in the merchant service, desired all ships to be manned in proportion to their registered tonnage, on the ground that ships ought not to be regarded as seaworthy if they are inadequately manned. But Mr. Raeburn, representing the Clyde District Committee of the Shipping Federation, considered any attempt to fix a manning scale at all to be "a vast mistake," because the number of hands required in proportion to the tonnage varied in inverse ratio with the size of the vessel.

Desertion,[1] formerly a criminal offence and punishable as such by fine or imprisonment, became, under the terms of section 10 of the Act of 1880, amenable only to a civil action for damages. All the shipowners' representatives complained that the abolition of the punishment of imprisonment had, in effect, deprived them of all protection against desertions. Theoretically, they could get damages from the offenders, but, practically, they could not, because seamen had no money to pay. Sir Henry Calcraft, however, declared that the re-imposition of the penalty of imprisonment for mere desertion was a sheer impossibility; but at the same time he pointed out that a seaman accepting an advance note with the deliberate intention of neglecting to join his ship was still liable criminally for obtaining money under false pretences.

Deck cargoes[2] were illegal from 1839 to 1862, when by a repeal of sections 170, 171, and 172 of the Customs Consolidation Act they were once more

---

[1] B. I. Dig. pp. 68, 69 ; B. II. Dig. pp. 114-117.
[2] B. I. Dig. p. 69 ; B. II. Dig. pp. 117-121.

permitted. In 1876, however, the prohibition was revived in the case of timber conveyed during the winter months from foreign or colonial to home ports, with an exception in favour of light wood goods to the height of three feet above the deck. In the opinion of Messrs. J. Havelock Wilson and S. Plimsoll, the safety of the seamen demanded greater stringency, and they accordingly proposed to abolish deck loading on all ships, both British and foreign, within the jurisdiction, during the winter months. Mr. Wilson further proposed to apply the three feet limit to summer voyages, while Mr. Plimsoll desired to deal with out-going vessels by making the issue of clearance papers contingent upon the requirements of the law being satisfactorily carried out, and with incoming vessels by empowering the magistrates to confiscate all the timber carried illegally.

Rating of seamen [1] is regulated by section 7 of the Act of 1880, which provides that no seaman shall be entitled to the rating of an A.B., unless he has served four years before the mast, and that such service may be proved by the certificates of discharge, which shipowners are obliged, under section 172 of the Act of 1854, to give every seaman on leaving their service. Mr. J. Havelock Wilson proposed to amend the law by providing for the exchange of these discharges for parchment certificates of competency, similar to those issued to officers and obtainable by a practical examination, by making it a penal offence to employ as an A.B. a man unprovided with such a certificate, and by issuing similar certi-

[1] B. I. Dig. pp. 69, 70 ; B. II. Dig. pp. 121-3.

ficates under similar conditions to firemen, cooks, and stewards.

Watertight compartments[1] were formerly provided for by section 300 of the Act of 1854, which enacted that no steamer was to be allowed to clear unless she had one iron bulkhead before, and another iron bulkhead abaft the engine-room, but, by section 2 of the Act of 1862, the former enactment was repealed. Mr. Plimsoll contended that it was not sufficient to trust entirely to the owners' personal interests for the safety of merchant vessels, on account of the practice of over-insurance, and that section 300 of the Act of 1854 ought to be re-enacted. On the other hand, Mr. Scrutton, representing the Chamber of Shipping of the United Kingdom, explained that the section was repealed because it had been rendered obsolete by the stricter regulations of Lloyds', and by the voluntary efforts of the shipowners themselves, while Mr. Raeburn, representing the Clyde District Committee of the Shipping Federation, declared that systematic over-insurance would be "a decidedly losing game," and was, in fact, never practised.

Presence of unauthorised persons[2] on board ship is subject to the rules laid down in section 5 of the Merchant Seamen (Payment of Wages and Rating) Act, 1880, which forbids such persons from entering a vessel on its arrival at a port, without the permission of the master. In order to prevent Union delegates entering the ships and tempting the crew to break their agreements, Mr. G. A. Laws, representing the

[1] B. II. Dig. p. 123.
[2] B. I. Dig. p. 69.

Shipping Federation, wished this provision to be extended to vessels on the point of departure.

Special regulations are also applied to barges, public carriages and railways in virtue of the Canal Boats Acts, 1877 and 1884, the Metropolitan Public Carriages Act, 1869, and the Railway Regulation Acts.

The Canal Boats Acts, 1877 and 1884[1].—The proposals relating to the Canal Boats Acts were as follows :—(*a*) That certificates of competency should be required of all persons in charge of canal boats or lighters ; (*b*) that women and children should be prohibited from living or working on canal boats ; (*c*) that permission to children under 13 to work on canal boats should be limited to those that have passed the third educational standard ; (*d*) that Mr. Plimsoll's mark should be observed in all river craft ; (*e*) that the Acts should apply to all vessels concerned in inland navigation ; (*f*) that the registration of canal boats should be more uniform and systematic ; (*g*) that inspection should be periodical ; (*h*) that district sub-inspectors should be specially appointed for the administration of the Acts.

The Metropolitan Public Carriages Act, 1869[2].—In connection with this Act, the principal proposals were :— (*a*) To make the London County Council or the Board of Trade the licensing authority for metropolitan cabs and drivers ; (*b*) to enable the licensing authority to fix the price paid for cabs by drivers to proprietors ;

---

[1] B. II. Dig. pp. 124-8 ; B. III. pp. 137, 138.
[2] B. II. pp. 90, 91 ; B. III. pp. 38-44.

(c) to empower magistrates to deal summarily with cab thieves; (d) to repeal 46 Geo. III., c. 134, s. 35, forbidding cabs to ply for hire within 300 feet of any house in Bloomsbury Square; (e) to amend 6 and 7 Vict., c. 86, s. 38, by substituting £10 for £3 as the amount recoverable by proprietors from drivers for wilful damage to cabs; (f) to repeal 6 and 7 Vict., c. 86, s. 35, which makes proprietors liable to be called upon to produce drivers.

The Railway Regulation Acts[1].—The Act of 1893 provides that the Board of Trade, on receipt of a formal complaint from any determinate body of railway servants as to their excessive hours of labour, shall investigate the matter, and, if the grievance appears genuine, shall require the company to reduce their hours within reasonable limits. The secretary of the Railway Workers' Union, however, had informed the Commission that the members of the organisation he represented would be satisfied with nothing less than a legal 48 hours' week for all classes of workers. The representatives of the Amalgamated Society of Railway Servants, an older and more aristocratic organisation, were not so extreme in their views; but their policy also was somewhat in advance of the newly enacted Act of Parliament, and they made the following detailed proposal:—That, on application to the Board of Trade by a majority of the men employed in handling the traffic in the service or in any one grade of the service of any railway company, the

[1] B. III. pp. 48 and foll. ; App. 157.

O

following regulations should be enforced in respect of the applicants :—

I. The regulation of the hours of duty of railway men shall be such that the period of *ten hours* shall not be exceeded in any one day's work, nor shall those duties be resumed without there having been allowed *an interval of nine hours*, excepting in the case of accidents. Where meal hours are allowed, an hour may be deducted from the total of the day's work in those cases only where the workman has been for that period free to leave the railway company's premises and clear of all responsibilities and duties.

II. In the case of signalmen and pointsmen, the signal cabins shall be scheduled into three classes, the hours of duty in each class to be restricted as under :

(*a*) First class, not to exceed eight hours a day.

(*b*) Second class, not to exceed nine hours a day.

(*c*) Third class, not to exceed ten hours a day.

III. The hours on duty of men employed exclusively in the occupation of shunting shall not exceed eight hours a day. In the event of a railway company keeping a workman on duty beyond the prescribed number of hours, it shall pay such workman for the said overwork at twenty-five per centum over and above the rate of pay for the ordinary day's work. Any failure to comply with this requirement shall, on being proved to the Board of Trade, be met by an order of the Board of Trade enforcing such payment. In any case, where the day's work of a railway man exceeds *twelve* hours, it shall be reported to the Board of Trade, who shall inquire into the cause of the said overwork, and, unless the same be found to have occurred through some accident or other unforeseen occurrence beyond the control of the responsible officers of the railway company, the Board of Trade shall have power to impose a penalty on the company for the offence.

Proposals were also made concerning inquests, inspection, and certificates of competency for engine-drivers, on all of which points the men's representatives desired the law to be strengthened.

CHAPTER III.

AGRICULTURE.

The Agricultural Labour Programme—Is the Programme of the Town Labourers—The Assistant Commissioners' Reports— Supply of Labour—Conditions of Engagement—Wages and Earnings—Cottages—Land held by Agricultural Labourers —Benefit Societies—Relations between Employers and Employed—Trade Unions—General condition of the Agricultural Labourer.

THE inquiry into the condition of the agricultural labourer was entrusted by the Commission to a body of Assistant Commissioners, who were to visit thirty-eight selected districts and make their investigations on the spot. The Blue Books containing the result of their work have attracted a considerable amount of attention, and a summary of their contents by Mr. W. C. Little, the Senior Assistant Commissioner, has lately been issued.

Interesting and valuable as those Blue Books have proved themselves to be, they do not bear so directly upon the labour question as the evidence received by the Commission in Westminster Hall. For the problem consists mainly in the discovery of the nature and strength of workmen's demands. And the agricultural labourer is making no definite demands. Aspirations he has, and demands he is preparing to make; but, at present, he has no really effective industrial organisation and no clearly defined political programme.

Rural reforms, indeed, have a prominent place in the political programme of some of the urban Trade Unions, which desire to check the migration of the agricultural labourers to the towns, and to send the surplus town population into the country; and, with these ends in view, their representatives expressed themselves in favour of legislation to facilitate the acquisition of allotments, especially in the neighbourhood of seaport towns, the creation of parish councils with strong administrative powers, the establishment of farm colonies, etc., etc. But these demands are the outcome of the grievances of the town labourers, and furnish no indication of the real wants of the agricultural population.

The principal subjects dealt with in the Assistant Commissioners' Reports are as follows:—Supply of Labour, Conditions of Engagement, Wages and Earnings, Cottages, Land held by Agricultural Labourers, Benefit Societies, Relations between Employers and Employed, Trade Unions, and the General Condition of the Agricultural Labourer.

Supply of Labour.—In most parts of England, it appears that there is less demand for labour than formerly, owing to the increased use of machinery, the laying down of cultivated land to pasture, and the consolidation of farms; but this decrease in demand has been balanced by decrease in supply, owing to the migration to towns and the uprising of com-

peting local industries. Skilled farm labour, indeed,
is somewhat scarce in some districts, and the farmers
complain that the men's efficiency tends to deterio-
rate. In Wales, the supply of labour was said to be
never greater and often less than the demand, and
complaints were made of the growing tendency of the
men to be continually changing their employment
and abode. In Scotland, the supply of agricultural
labour was said to be much smaller, relatively to the
demand, than was the case twenty years ago, female
farm labour being at a specially high premium. In
Ireland, moreover, there seemed to be a general dearth
of labour during busy seasons, and, owing to emigration, the unwholesomeness of modern diet and the
depressed nature of the industry, a marked falling off
in its quality.

Conditions of Engagement.—In most parts of
England, it is the general practice to work the farms
with a regular staff engaged by the year, with
month's or quarter's notice, and to supplement it
during busy seasons with casual labour, often imported wholesale from the towns. In the Eastern
Counties, however, engagements are usually by the
day, or even by the hour, and regular work can
seldom be guaranteed. The hours of labour vary,
according to season and district, from eight to fourteen a-day, but ordinary labourers rarely work more
than eleven. Sunday work is for the most part
confined to those in charge of animals. In Wales,
engagements are generally by the year or half-year
for unmarried labourers boarding at the farm, and by

the week for married labourers. Employment is
almost always regular and continuous, the hours are
from sunrise to sunset, while Sunday work falls
chiefly upon the stockmen. In Scotland, engagements by the year or half-year are the rule for
married and unmarried labourers alike. Employment is regular, and casual labourers are few. In
some districts, where female labour is specially scarce,
every married man is expected to supply a woman to
work on the farm and give her board and lodging.
The hours of labour for all classes, except shepherds,
are possibly rather less than in England. The necessary Sunday work is generally performed by a few
persons taking their turn to work full time in order
to enable the majority to enjoy a complete day's rest.
With shepherds, cattlemen, and dairywomen, however, this system is often found impracticable. In
Ireland, engagements are for long periods and employment is regular in some districts, while, in others,
engagements are by the day or week, and employment
is intermittent. The greatest regularity is obtained
where tillage preponderates; but, where hay is the
principal crop, there is alternately an excessive demand for labour, and an excessive supply. The hours
are comparatively short, while Sunday work is very
limited.

Wages and Earnings.—Taking the whole of the
selected districts, the average weekly wage of carters
and stockmen is 14s. 8d., of shepherds, 15s. 8d., and
of ordinary labourers, 13s. 5d. The provisions of the
Truck Acts relating to payments in kind, how-

ever, are relaxed in the case of agricultural
labourers, or "servants in husbandry," as they are
technically called, and the wages are, consequently,
liable to large additions in the form of perquisites and
allowances. Although in every district there is a
tendency for payments in kind to disappear, their
present value is sufficient to raise the figures given
above, as follows :—Carters and stockmen, 17s. 2d.;
shepherds, 18s. 2d.; ordinary labourers, 15s. 11d.
Taking all these classes together, and making due
allowance for irregular employment, the average
annual earnings, per adult male, are £45, as against
an average for all classes of manual labourers in
the Kingdom of £60. The addition of the earnings
of women and children, moreover, raises the total
family earnings considerably. Owing to the men's
desire to be kept on during the winter and of the
farmers to maintain the supply of labour during the
summer, piecework is generally unpopular in high
wage districts, and, though not seldom preferred
where wages are low, is almost everywhere giving
way to time payments.

Cottages.—In Wales, Scotland and Ireland, it is still
the rule for labourers to live in detached cottages on
the farms where they are employed, or even in their
employers' houses. But throughout the Kingdom
there is a growing tendency to migrate from farm
cottages to hamlets, and from hamlets to villages, and,
in England, village life is certainly the rule. The
internal condition of the cottages varies; but everywhere there seems to be a distinct tendency towards

improvement, and, rents being generally low, it is only
very seldom that the tenants are not receiving full
value for their money.   Other things being equal, the
labourers like to live off their employers' and their
employers' landlords' estates, so as not to be obliged
to hold their cottages actually or virtually on tenure
of employment.   Both farmers and squires are, accordingly, obliged to provide improved cottage accommodation in order to compete with the speculative
builders, whose cottages the labourers would otherwise
prefer.

Land held by Agricultural Labourers.—Although
the Allotment Acts have certainly increased the
number of allotments taken by the labourers in some
districts, they have been almost entirely inoperative
in Wales, Scotland, Ireland, and many parts of England, while, in most English counties, the supply of
allotments seems to be considerably in excess of the
demand.   Gardens and potato grounds attached to
cottages are appreciated and well cultivated in some
districts; but, in many, such is by no means the case.

Benefit Societies.—Friendly and benefit societies of
various kinds are well supported in England, where
there is a tendency for the larger and sounder concerns,
like the Ancient Order of Foresters, to swallow up
the smaller ones.   In Wales, where the smaller
societies prevail to a greater extent, and where the
money invested is less secure, they are not so well
supported.   In Scotland, labourers whose wages are
" upstanding " seldom support any benefit society;
but some institutions, such as the Prudential Life

Insurance Society, have a considerable membership,
Among the Irish agricultural labourers, benefit societies can hardly be said to be supported at all, except
the burial societies, which seem everywhere to have a
peculiar attraction for the poorest classes.

Relations between Employers and Employed.—The
agricultural labourers do not yet seem to have defined
their attitude towards their employers in any way of
which the Assistant Commissioners could take special
cognisance, and their reports on this head afford but
hazy information in consequence. Symptoms of
antagonism, however, reveal themselves in the complaints of the farmers that the workmen are "more
independent than formerly and less ready to oblige."

Trade Unions.—Trade Unionism among agricultural labourers has hitherto been of a very tentative
and spasmodic character. It made some headway
under Mr. Joseph Arch in the seventies, but most of
the organisations he caused to be founded began to
decline as soon as the first excitement had evaporated.
The movement was revived by the missionaries of the
Dockers' and other urban Trade Unions in 1890, but
the organisations then founded or resuscitated did
not succeed in securing a permanent footing, and
are, for the most part, inactive, dwindling, and
dormant. At present, organisation in England is
chiefly represented by the National Agricultural
Labourers' Union and the Eastern Counties' Federation, both of which are particularly strong in Essex.
In Scotland, the Ploughmen's Federal Union is

struggling hard to obtain a footing, and is apparently meeting with a moderate degree of success. In Ireland and Wales, however, organisation can nowhere be said to do more than tend to exist. Rural Trade Unions are discussed and promoted, but they do not live and act, and the same statement may, broadly, be said to hold good for the United Kingdom as a whole. Each successive movement, however, has left behind it the seeds of stronger and nobler successors. The momentary tendency to decay is only part of a general tendency towards more vigorous life.

General Condition of the Agricultural Labourer.— Economic laws prevent the material condition of agricultural labourers being very far behind that of their brethren in the towns. Improvement in the conditions of town labour and life causes the best men to leave the country, and appreciates the labour of those that remain. So it happens that falling prices of agricultural produce, and diminishing agricultural rents and profits, have been accompanied by rising agricultural wages. And all the other material conditions, under which the rural labourer lives and works, have improved in proportion. The Assistant Commissioners concurred in reporting that he was, on the whole, and in most districts, better fed, better clothed and better housed than he ever was before, and quoted the expressed opinions of landowners, farmers, clergy, and the labourers themselves to the same effect.

At the same time, the reports show the material condition of the agricultural labourer to be still inferior to that of most other workmen. His wages are 25 per cent. below the average for the United Kingdom, and his general mode of living is lower in proportion. His principal grievance, however, appears to be a metaphysical one. For the Reports are full of complaints of the lack of cheap rational amusements in the country, and state the great bugbear of rural life to be not so much its poverty as its intolerable dulness.

The dependence of the agricultural labourer upon his employer away from his work is another great grievance. His master is often his landlord, and a person with whom he dare not quarrel for fear of losing his home. As a Gloucestershire labourer told the Assistant Commissioner who visited the district, " In only too many cases, a man's home and work are so bound together that he has not the liberty, which is essential to the progress he would otherwise endeavour to make."[1]

Discontent, based on metaphysical and non-material wants, is a sure token of awakened self-consciousness. And from conscious feeling to conscious endeavour is but a single step. In the meantime, however, the Labour Movement can hardly be said to reach what still remains the principal industry of the country.

[1] Reports on the Agricultural Labourer, vol. i., part iv. (District Report, No. ii., pars. 67 and 68).

CHAPTER IV.

LABOUR DEPARTMENTS AND LABOUR COUNCILS.

The Labour Department of the Board of Trade—Its Statistical
Functions—Its proposed Administrative Functions—Con-
sultative Labour Councils—The French Higher Council of
Labour—The Belgian Higher Council of Labour.

BEFORE the Commission had concluded its sittings for
the purpose of taking evidence, the new Labour
Department was formed, or rather the existing Labour
Department of the Board of Trade was placed in a
quasi-independent position with slightly extended
functions and a larger staff. Like the Labour Department of the United States, it merely collects and
publishes facts and figures ; but there was nothing in
the evidence to indicate that Mr. Mundella's reforms
would not prove amply sufficient to meet the demand
for improved industrial statistics.

The principal demand, however, was for improved
administrative machinery, and, as has been seen in the
preceding chapters, several witnesses desired the new
Department to act as a Central Labour Exchange, to
assume the administration of the laws relating to
mines and factories, and to arbitrate in trade disputes.
But, here again, there was nothing in the evidence to

show that such administrative functions would be better discharged by an inexperienced staff than by the existing administrative authorities.

At the same time, the frequent appointment of expensive temporary Commissions is in itself a proof that, though the fault is neither in the statistical nor in the administrative departments, the permanent official machinery is in some respect defective. The idea of a Labour Department—not as a statistical or administrative—but as a permanent consultative body, has hitherto been overlooked.

Consultative Labour Councils of the nature of permanent Royal Commissions exist in France and Belgium, and, though of recent formation, afford interesting object lessons, as may be gathered from the following passages in the reports prepared by the Secretary to the Commission on the Labour Question in those countries.

"On January 22nd, 1891," he writes, "a decree was promulgated by the President of the French Republic, which established a Higher Council of Labour under the direction of the Minister of Commerce, Industry, and the Colonies. The composition of the Council, consisting as it does of only sixteen workmen, out of fifty members, has unfortunately aroused the hostility of the workmen's syndicates (Trade Unions) and of the Socialists, who consider it essential that the majority of the Council should be themselves workmen, and be directly nominated by workmen."[1]

"A despatch was annexed to the decree explaining that the Council was designed as a permanent instru-

[1] "Foreign Reports," vol. vi., France, pp. 89, 90.

ment for examining proposals, and preparing solutions on which Parliament might be required to pronounce, its object being to furnish rapidly and correctly such information respecting labour questions as had previously been obtained only after costly inquiries, the result of which had not corresponded to the effort made."

" The chief work of the first meeting was to define the functions of the Council, and to appoint special sub-committees for the consideration and investigation of special and pressing questions. These questions were :—

" 1st. Arbitration in trade disputes.
" 2nd. Labour registries.
" 3rd. Laws relating to wages, etc.
" 4th. Institution of a statistical labour department.

And a decree was published on August 21st, 1891, embodying many of the recommendations of the Council on these points."

" The second report of the Higher Council on Labour was published in November, 1892, containing recommendations on the following subjects :—

" 1st. Artisans' dwellings.
" 2nd. Establishment of a permanent committee to consider associations for popular credit.
" 3rd. The law relating to co-operative societies.
" 4th. The formation of a museum of social economy.
" 5th. The censorship of the Conseils de Prud' hommes over factory and workshop rules."

Referring to the Belgian Council,[1] moreover, the Secretary writes :—" A Higher Council of Labour was instituted at Brussels by two royal decrees of April 7th, 1892. The Council is a consultative body, whose duty it is to prepare questions for submission to the various councils of industry, and to present to the Government general proposals embodying their wishes. Questions relating to apprenticeship, technical education, workshop regulations, the measures to be taken to ensure the proper sanitation and safety of industrial establishments, the organisation of insurance against accidents, strikes and lock-outs, and legislation on trade contracts, come within the jurisdiction of the Council. It is organised on a basis analogous to that of the Higher Councils of Commerce, Industry, and Agriculture, and, like them, its business is to discuss questions submitted to it by the Government, to provide information respecting all labour questions, and to draft Bills for submission to the Legislature. When authorised by the Minister, it also deliberates on questions initiated by its own members."

" The Council consists of 48 members, 16 of whom represent the employers, 16 the employed, while 16 are other persons who have special knowledge of economic and social questions. The first members were appointed by the Government for four years; after that period, the representatives of the employers and employed are to be elected by the various Councils of Industry. The Council draws up rules for its own management, and is governed by a Board consisting of a President, three Vice-Presidents, and a Secretary.

[1] "Foreign Reports," vol. iv., Belgium, p. 39.

It has power to form one or more sections for certain functions ; but the President, senior Vice-President, and Secretary are members of each section. The Council classifies the matters submitted to it, and determines the order and method of its labours and discussions. All questions are decided by an absolute majority, and, in case of an equality of votes, the motion is considered lost. No resolution can be taken, unless at least half of the members are present. Each member receives 6 francs for every meeting which he attends."

" 'The first question submitted to the Council was the application of articles 4, 6, and 7 of the law of December 13th, 1889, respecting the labour of young men, women, and children in industrial establishments. At its first session, on May 18th, 1892, the Council divided its members into three sections for the consideration of this question in the various industries. The first section comprised mines, quarries, metals, the manufacture of machines, glass-making, pottery, and transport. The second dealt with clothing and textile industries. And the third took building trades, chemical and artistic industries, and those connected with the supply of food. Twenty sessions were held between May and November to discuss the reports of the Councils of Industry, convoked by a royal decree, on March 20th, for the consideration of this question. Five sessions of the whole Council were held in October and November, 1892, when the conclusions arrived at were discussed. The propositions of the Councils were submitted to the permanent provincial committees, by which they were, with the exception

P

of a few details, adopted unanimously, and they were
subsequently promulgated as royal decrees on December 26th and 31st, 1892."

CHAPTER V.

Strikes and Lockouts—Arbitration—Hours of Labour—Employers' Liability—The Factory Acts, etc.—State and Municipal Employment—The Unemployed—Mines—Transport Trades—Agriculture—The Labour Department.

As the result of its inquiries, the Commission has issued a Blue Book containing two principal reports, one signed by nineteen and the other by four of its members. Following the arrangement adopted in the preceding chapters, the recommendations contained in those Reports may be briefly summarised as follows :—

With reference to Strikes and Lockouts, the majority of the Commission recommend the amendment of Section 7 of the Conspiracy and Protection of Property Act, 1875, relating to picketing, so as to read —" Uses *or threatens to use* violence to such other person,"—instead of—" Uses violence to *or intimidates* such other person."

With reference to Arbitration, the majority desire to empower municipal and county councils to establish industrial courts to decide questions arising out of existing contracts or trade customs; to give one of the central Government Departments an adequate staff with adequate means to procure,

227

record, and circulate information relating to the work
of voluntary conciliation boards, and, by advice and
assistance, to promote their more rapid and universal
establishment ; and to give a public department, on
receipt of a sufficient application from the parties
interested or from local conciliation boards, power to
appoint a suitable person to act as arbitrator, either
alone or in conjunction with local boards or with
assessors appointed by the employers and workmen
concerned.

On the other hand, the minority consider that it
would be more advisable to grant adequate power
to the Labour Department to obtain the fullest
possible information about the facts of every dispute,
the actual net wages earned, the cost of living, the
price of the product, the cost of manufacture, the
salaries and interest paid, the employer's profit, and
such other details as may seem material.

With reference to Hours of Labour, the majority
desire to give a Secretary of State power to regulate
the hours of labour in any industry which he may
certify to be, in his opinion, dangerous or injurious to
health.   Such orders, they consider, should be final, if
protected persons (i.e., women, young persons, and
children) are concerned ; but, as regards adult males,
they should lie for a certain time upon the tables of
both Houses of Parliament before becoming law.

On the other hand, the minority recommend that
an Eight Hours Act should be passed, laying down
the principle of a maximum working-day, and author-
ising its application to particular industries, after due
inquiry, by the Home Secretary, in default of a
special Minister for Labour, with a view to the ulti-

mate securing of an eight hours day for every manual worker.

With reference to Employers' Liability, the minority declare that the Bill passed by the House of Commons but rejected by the House of Lords in 1893, embodied the reforms which they were disposed to recommend. They add that they are utterly opposed to any wage-earner being allowed to " contract out " in return for some individual advantage—a privilege contrary, as they assert, to the whole principle of our industrial legislation.

With reference to the Factory Acts, etc., the majority consider that an Act should be passed compelling every owner of workshops to obtain a certificate of the fitness of his premises and of the workshops of out-workers to be used for industrial purposes, especially in the case of manufacturers of clothing, boots, and cheap furniture, and in bakehouses and laundries. And they further recommend the amendment of the Factory Acts so as to enable young persons to be prohibited from working overtime in certain trades, *e.g.* in dressmaking, the extension of their provisions relating to sanitation and the employment of young persons to laundries, and the institution of a special Government inquiry into the confusion now existing in the administration of the various Acts relating to labour protection.

On the other hand, the minority desire to make employers whose work is performed in domestic workshops equally responsible for the sanitary, edu-cational and industrial well-being of their work-people as employers whose work is performed in regular factories and workshops; to reduce the legal

56½ hours limit per week to 48, and make it the law for all textile factories whether protected persons are employed therein or only adult males; to compel occupiers of all workplaces and landlords of all houses intended to be used or known to themselves to be used for industrial purposes to send a notification of the fact to the Factory Department; to largely increase the number of working-men sub-inspectors, and to give every inspector an office in every large industrial centre and an adequate clerical staff; to make better provision for the medical inspection of persons employed in factories and workshops by the appointment of a medical expert on the staff of the Department, to whom the certifying surgeons might send periodical reports; to appoint a small commission of medical and scientific experts to deal in succession with each of the industries in which the death-rate is above the average; to increase the number of female factory inspectors; to absolutely prohibit the employment of women in the more dangerous portions of the white lead manufacture; and to sever the connection of the Factory Department with the Home Office. The adoption of these recommendations, they assert, would involve a cost ' not exceeding £50,000 a year.

With reference to State and Municipal employment, the minority recommend the explicit and widely advertised adoption by all public bodies of direct public employment, the eight hours day, Trade Union conditions and a moral minimum wage of at least 21s. a week; the express binding of public contractors, where such are employed, to adopt the same conditions; the establishment of a Dock and

Harbour Board composed of representatives of the London County Council, the Town Council of West Ham and other public bodies concerned, of the ship-owners and of the dock labourers, with power to take over and administer the dock and wharves below London Bridge, and to discharge all the present functions of the Thames Conservancy, at any rate as regards the lower 'navigation ; and the undertaking by the new Board of an inquiry into the scheme for concentrating the London Docks submitted by Mr. Tom Mann.

With reference to the Unemployed, the majority consider that public authorities should hold over-work needed, but not urgent, with a view to furnishing employment in times of depression.

On the other hand, the minority recommend the undertaking of public works of a useful, though not necessarily of a remunerative character, full wages being paid to those employed, and no stigma of pauperism being attached to those relieved ; the experimental establishment of Labour Colonies ; and the grant of old age pensions in the manner suggested by Mr. C. Booth.

With reference to Mines, the minority recommend the passing of the Eight Hours Bill into law and the increase of the inspectoral staff by the addition of practical working miners or miners' agents.

With reference to Transport Trades, the majority recommend the amendment of the law, so that the wives of seamen should receive their husbands' pay *fortnightly* on their allotment notes to the extent of *one-half* of the pay due.

On the other hand, the minority recommend the

amendment of the law, so that the wives of seamen should receive their husband's pay *weekly* on their allotment notes to the extent of *two-thirds* of the pay due; the systematic inspection of provisions on all British ships; the enforcement of a manning scale, so adjusted as to secure a normal eight hours day for sailors and firemen; the restriction of the employment of non-European seamen to a limited proportion of the crew; the provision of at least 120 feet of cubic space in the seamen's sleeping-places; and the direct election by the seamen registered as residing at each port of representatives to sit on the Local Marine Boards.

With reference to Agriculture, the minority recommend Parliament to confer upon Parish Councils in Great Britain the same power of providing cottages as is enjoyed by Boards of Guardians in Ireland, and by Town Councils throughout the Kingdom; and to make compulsory the Labourers (Ireland) Act, 1881.

With reference, finally, to the functions of the Labour Department, the majority recommend the engagement under its auspices of a staff of skilled investigators to inquire into the conditions of labour, and the formation of a census of occupations.

On the other hand, the minority recommend the formation of a new Department of Labour in which should be included the present Factory and Mines Departments of the Home Office, the Labour Department of the Board of Trade, and the Registry of Friendly Societies; the creation of a special Minister for Labour, with a seat in the Cabinet; and the grant of additional power to the Labour Department to obtain the fullest possible information about industrial matters.

In addition to these Reports, the Blue Book contains separate statements of the individual views of certain members of the Commission. Of these, the most comprehensive is the statement of Sir John Gorst, who failed to sign either of the principal Reports. He recommends the appointment by local public bodies of local industrial boards, composed of employers and employed in equal numbers, before which parties to disputes should be compelled to state their cases before resorting to strikes or lock-outs; the legislative regulation of the hours of labour in all industrial undertakings protected or patronised by Government, or where the conditions of labour are specially dangerous or unhealthy; the extension of employers' liability to cases of pure accident and the prohibition of "contracting out"; and the concentration of all administrative governmental functions relating to industry in a single Department.

Mr. Jesse Collings, moreover, advocates the advance to landowners by the State of loans to enable them to place agricultural labourers in possession of small holdings. But by far the most important proposal contained in the supplementary Reports is that made by the Duke of Devonshire to the effect that Trade Unions and Employers' Associations, instead of being controlled by section 4 of the Trade Union Act, 1871, should be enabled to acquire some of the rights and liabilities of corporate bodies. In making this proposal, the Chairman is supported by several of his colleagues.

APPENDIX.

LIST OF PUBLICATIONS

(With the Prices)

ISSUED BY THE ROYAL COMMISSION ON LABOUR.

REPORTS.

Reference Number.	Title.	Price. s.	d.
[C. 6708.]	First Report - - - - -	0	0½
[C. 6795.]	Second Report - - - -	0	0½
[C. 6894.]	Third Report - - - - -	0	0½
[C. 7063.]	Fourth Report - - - -	0	0½
[C. .]	Fifth and Final Report, Part I. -	2	6
[C. .]	Fifth and Final Report, Part II. -	6	0

MINUTES OF EVIDENCE.[1]

[C. 6708—IV.]	Minutes of Evidence, with Appendices, taken before Group A., Vol. I.	3	10½
[C. 6795—IV.]	Vol. II. - - - - -	5	3
[C. 6894—VII.]	Vol. III. - - - - -	5	0
[C. 6708—V.]	Minutes of Evidence, with Appendices, taken before Group B., Vol. I.	5	9
[C. 6795—V.]	Vol. II. - - - - -	3	6
[C. 6894—VIII.]	Vol. III. - - - -	9	10

[1] The whole of the Minutes of Evidence is also published in detached portions at the price of 2d. for each day's evidence, or, with postage, 3d. or 3½d.

234

DIGESTS OF EVIDENCE.

ANSWERS TO SCHEDULES AND RULES OF ASSOCIATIONS.

Reference Number.	Title.	Price. s. d.
[C. 7063—IX.]	Vol. VI.—France - - -	2 1
[C. 7063—X.]	Vol. VII.—Switzerland - - -	0 5
[C. 7063—XII.]	Vol. VIII.—Italy - - -	0 11
[C. 7063—XIII.]	Vol. IX.—Denmark, Sweden and Norway, Spain and Portugal -	0 6½
[C. 7063—XIV.]	Vol. X.—Russia - - - -	0 7½
[C. 7063—XI.]	Vol. XI.—Austria-Hungary and the Balkan States - - - -	2 11

REPORT ON THE EMPLOYMENT OF WOMEN.

[C. 6894—XXIII.] The Employment of Women—Reports by Miss Eliza Orme, Miss Clara E. Collet, Miss May E. Abraham, and Miss Margaret H. Irwin on the Conditions of Work in various Industries -   -   - 2 10

REPORTS ON THE AGRICULTURAL LABOURER.

[C. 6894—I.] The Agricultural Labourer, Vol. I., England, Part I.—Reports by Mr. William E. Bear upon certain Selected Districts in the Counties of Bedford, Hampshire, Huntingdon, Leicester, Nottingham, and Sussex -   -   -   -   - 1 3

[C. 6894—II.] Part II.—Reports by Mr. Cecil M. Chapman upon certain Selected Districts in the Counties of Berkshire, Buckinghamshire, Cambridgeshire, Cornwall, Devonshire, Hertfordshire, Oxfordshire, and Shropshire -   -   -   - 1 4

[C. 6894—III.] Part III.—Reports by Mr. Arthur Wilson Fox upon certain Selected Districts in the Counties of Cumberland, Lancashire, Norfolk, Northumberland, and Suffolk   - 1 5

Reference Number.	Title.	Price. s. d.

[C. 6894—IV.] Part IV.—Reports by Mr. Roger C. Richards upon certain Selected Districts in the Counties of Cheshire, Derbyshire, Gloucestershire, Herefordshire, Monmouthshire, Northamptonshire, and Warwickshire - - - - 1 0

[C. 6894—V.] Part V.—Reports by Mr. Aubrey J. Spencer upon certain Selected Districts in the Counties of Dorset, Essex, Kent, Somerset, Surrey, Wilts, and Worcester - - 1 0

[C. 6894—VI.] Part VI.—Reports by Mr. Edward Wilkinson upon certain Selected Districts in the Counties of Derbyshire, Lincolnshire, Staffordshire, and Yorkshire (N.E. and W. Riding) - - - - - - 1 0

[C. 6894—XIII.] Part VII.—Indexes (Analytical and General) - - - - - 0 8½

[C. 6894—XIV.] The Agricultural Labourer, Vol. II., Wales.—Reports by Mr. D. Lleufer Thomas upon certain Selected Districts in the Counties of Anglesey, Carmarthen, Carnarvon, Denbigh, Glamorgan, Merioneth, Montgomery, and Pembroke, to which is added a Report by Mr. C. M. Chapman upon a Selected District in the Counties of Brecon and Radnor ; with Analytical and General Indexes - - - 1 8

[C. 6894—XV.] The Agricultural Labourer, Vol. III., Scotland, Part I.—Reports by Mr. H. Rutherford, and by the late Mr. G. R. Gillespie, upon certain Selected Districts in the Counties of Aberdeen, Argyll (South), Ayr, Banff, Bute, Caith-

Reference Number.	Title.	Price. s. d.
	ness, Dumbarton, Dumfries, Forfar, Kincardine, Kirkcudbright, Lanark (North), Linlithgow, Moray, Nairn, Orkney, Perth (East), Renfrew, Ross, Stirling, Sutherland, and Wigtown - - -	1 4
[C. 6894—xvi.]	Part II.—Reports by Mr. R. Hunter Pringle and Mr. Edward Wilkinson upon certain Selected Districts in the Counties of Berwick, Clackmannan, Edinburgh, Fife, Haddington, Kinross, the Arable District between Inverness and Dingwall, and in North Uist, the Hill Districts of Selkirk, Peebles, and Dumfries, the Pastoral District of Breadalbane in Perth, and the Borders of Inverness and Ross-shire - - - - - -	1 9
[C. 6894—xvii.]	Part III.—Indexes (Analytical and General) - - - - -	0 4
[C. 6894—xviii.]	The Agricultural Labourer, Vol. IV., Ireland, Part I.—Reports by Mr. R. McCrea upon certain Selected Districts in Counties Antrim, Armagh, Donegal, Down, Fermanagh, Leitrim, Londonderry, Longford, Louth, Meath, Monaghan, Sligo, Tyrone, and Westmeath - - - - -	1 1
[C. 6894—xix.]	Part II.—Reports by Mr. W. P. O'Brien, C.B., upon certain Selected Districts in Counties Carlow, Cork, Clare, Kerry, Kildare, Kilkenny, King's, Limerick, Queen's, Tipperary, Waterford, Wexford, and Wicklow - -	1 4
[C. 6894—xx.]	Part III.—Reports by Mr. Roger C. Richards upon certain Selected	

Reference Number.	Title.	Price. s. d.
	Districts in the Counties of Cavan, Dublin, Galway, and Tipperary -	0 7½
[C. 6894—xxi.]	Part IV.—Reports by Mr. Arthur Wilson Fox (Assistant Commissioner), upon certain Selected Districts in the Counties of Cork, Mayo, Roscommon, and Westmeath - - - - -	1 2
[C. 6894—xxii.]	Part V.—Indexes (Analytical and General) - - - - -	0 6
[C. 6894—xxiii.]	The Agricultural Labourer, Vol. V., General Report, by Mr. Wm. C. Little (Senior Assistant Agricultural Commissioner.) (*Two volumes in preparation*) - -	—

INDEX.

.